I'D LIKE TO
BELIEVE

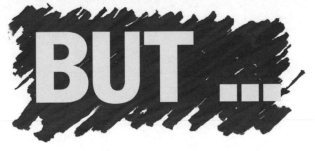

BUT ...

MICHAEL GREEN
& NICK SPENCER

I'D LIKE TO
BELIEVE
BUT ...

ivp

INTER-VARSITY PRESS
Norton Street, Nottingham NG7 3HR, England
Email: ivp@ivpbooks.com
Website: www.ivpbooks.com

First published 2005
Reprinted 2006
This edition 2009

British Library Cataloguing in Publication Data
A catalogue record for this book is available from the British Library.

ISBN 978-1-84474-390-2

Set in Monotype Dante 12/15pt
Typeset in Great Britain by Servis Filmsetting Ltd, Stockport, Cheshire
Printed and bound in Great Britain by Ashford Colour Press Ltd, Gosport, Hampshire

Inter-Varsity Press publishes Christian books that are true to the Bible and that communicate the gospel, develop discipleship and strengthen the church for its mission in the world.

Inter-Varsity Press is closely linked with the Universities and Colleges Christian Fellowship, a student movement connecting Christian Unions in universities and colleges throughout Great Britain, and a member movement of the International Fellowship of Evangelical Students. Website: www.uccf.org.uk

CONTENTS

INTRODUCTION – *BEYOND BELIEF?*

I was fascinated when I saw the slender volume, *Beyond Belief?* It is a research project into people's current beliefs conducted by Nick Spencer and published in 2003. I have not been able to leave it alone. I could not help myself. I knew I had to respond to it.

Beyond Belief? is extraordinarily illuminating. Nick is a researcher who at that time worked for a very forward-looking organization, the London Institute for Contemporary Christianity. (He now works for Theos, the Christian think-tank.) He does not generalize about attitudes in contemporary Britain. He will have nothing to do with the over-simplifications which are commonplace in popular discussions of postmodernism and its effect on religion. Here is a serious market researcher, taking the trouble to interview and discover the views of agnostics, who actually represent the mainstream of our population.

How Nick organized his research is explained in the appendix. The main points for us to notice at this stage are as follows. Those he interviewed are thoroughly representative.* They do not go to church. They are unsure about God for a variety of reasons. Some would still call themselves Christians. Others would not. Bearing in mind the large proportion of the country they represent (66% according to the Office of National Statistics), his survey is therefore highly relevant to the social fabric of the nation and, of course, to the strategy of the church.

I have long been intrigued by the different faces of

---

* All interviewees' names have been changed to protect identities.

unbelief, and I was immediately attracted to the results of this survey. By their own definition the respondents were agnostic, and it is very instructive to examine their objections to Christian belief. Some of these objections were substantial and far-reaching, but many were disappointingly weak and confused. It reminded me how far most people in this country are from having any real understanding of the Christian faith. But the climate of the day draws them into rejecting the faith that many of them have never examined. Here are some quotations, derived from Nick's researches, which show the spiritual hunger that most people have. They are expressed in much the same way, irrespective of age, gender or location, and they show a longing to believe – if only belief could be credible!

- 'My head tells me there isn't a God, but my heart wants to believe in it.'
- 'Well, I suppose you could go to science and dismiss God altogether, but I think there is some sort of supreme power that is shaping our world – but what, I don't know.'
- 'I think people who say they are atheist have not thought about it. It is a massive statement to make. I think these days people find it difficult to relate to most religions, not just Christianity.'
- 'I'd like to believe that there is a greater being of some description, but I don't know that I do believe in him.'
- 'I can't be clear about whether there is a God. I find that very difficult to be absolutely sure about, but I do feel there is some kind of existence after we die.'

- 'Without having that higher plane or greater being, you'd never have hope. Hope would be pointless.'
- 'Without that hope what have you got? Nothing to look forward to. So, what is the point of life? A lot of people see it like that.'
- 'I refuse to believe that you are born, you live, you die, and that's it.'
- 'I always wanted to believe it, but I can't from an intellectual point of view.'
- 'I would love to believe. That is my whole thing. I would love to believe, but however hard I try or don't try, I have never had any kind of sign to me personally.'

In a word, what many of these respondents are saying is *'I'd like to believe, but . . .'* I have written this book to try to remove some of those 'buts'. For it is to address questions like these, so honest, so open, so spiritually hungry, that our Christian gospel exists. Real Christianity makes sense of our questions, our longings and our doubts.

My heart goes out to the thousands of people who are struggling with issues like these, who feel there is no solid ground on which they can stand. I am confident that there is solid ground. I hope that will become clear in the chapters that follow, as we look at a number of characteristic difficulties in belief which people hold.

As Nick and I talked, we were convinced that this should be a joint production. At the outset of each chapter, Nick has fleshed out the responses he received, giving the personal background which he knew, but of which I, having had no part in the research, was completely ignorant. I then attempt to respond to the difficulties raised by his respondent. Nick then made many helpful suggestions about my responses! We hope that this joint book will be a help, both to those open-minded agnostics who form such a large proportion of our population, and to those Christians who want to connect with them.

Michael Green
Oxford Centre for Christian Apologetics, 2009

1. 'YOU DON'T NEED TO GO TO CHURCH TO BE SPIRITUAL'

Melanie is 50, married, and lives in the suburbs with her husband and two children. She considers herself to be a spiritual person and is open to mystical experiences.

She has tried yoga and various types of meditation over the years but doesn't practise with any regularity today. She believes in the existence of ghosts, although she has never seen one herself. She reads her horoscope in the paper religiously.

An intelligent and trusted friend of hers had an out-of-body experience a couple of years ago and this bolstered her sense of the divine, although she clearly feels uncomfortable talking about 'God'. Instead she prefers phrases such as 'something else', 'somewhere else' or 'another plane' and likes to talk about 'spiritual energy'.

Melanie had a token Christian upbringing. Her parents were nominal Anglicans and she attended Sunday school for a few years before the family moved house. Her knowledge of Christianity is, by her own admission, a bit shaky, but she definitely sees herself as a Christian. She wrote 'Christian' on her 2001 National Census form and puts 'Church of England' down whenever she is filling in forms on behalf of her children.

That said, she is pretty much indifferent to the church. She enjoys the occasional Christmas or harvest service and even attended her local parish church semi-regularly a few years back when her children were involved with scouts and guides. She was never really committed, however, partly because her association was primarily through her children but mainly because she found the 'narrowness' of it all rather off-putting.

'I think people can be extremely spiritual and have not

necessarily committed themselves,' she says. The idea that spirituality is bigger than the church is a recurring theme in what she says.

'You can talk, pray, anytime, all the time, wherever, it doesn't matter.' When asked about how she and other people might relate to God (a concept with which, somewhat surprisingly, she is perfectly comfortable), she says, 'I don't think you have to go to church to relate to him. If you believe in him he is always there for you and overlooking you.'

When pressed on the issue, she admits that it is possible to be spiritual in church but unlikely. 'The established church . . . is built on rites and rituals', she explains. 'It has so much dogma that I think [it] could be tried in a court of justice and could be found guilty of killing off spirituality.'

She has no objection to Christianity, as such, but nor does she see its need. Far better, she thinks, to practise your faith quietly, personally and unobtrusively. 'You can pray in the garden,' she says, 'but you can't do the gardening in a church.'

Response

Melanie, I have a lot of sympathy with what you have expressed. You represent millions in our country who see things the same way. So let me show some of the areas where we agree.

First, I like the fresh and natural way in which you express your spirituality. For the past two centuries, ever since the eighteenth-century Enlightenment when people rejected God and enthroned Reason in his place, human spirituality has been crushed. It has, of course, sometimes erupted in such places as the Romantic poets, like Keats and Wordsworth. I should not be surprised if, like many of us, you had to read Keats' *Ode to a Nightingale* or Wordsworth's

Daffodils when you were at school, and were touched by their warmth and spirituality. But these men, and the Romantic Movement they represented, were exceptions. The main thrust of European thought was dominated by science: only what we can touch and measure is real. Emotions are unreliable and unimportant. Well, in an atmosphere like that, spirituality cannot flourish. It retires into the shell of our private feelings and does not dare to emerge into the market-place of ideas.

But all that has been changing fast in the last thirty years or so. A growing disenchantment has set in with the emotionless, dehumanizing tendencies of a narrowly scientific approach. What is more, people are worried because science, as well as giving us unprecedented benefits, has produced the nuclear bomb and the power to blow the world sky high. An equal disenchantment has emerged with the pressures of the workplace which had no interest in people's feelings – but only in their productivity. We have begun to get in touch with our feelings again, and we value them highly. After all, these are the really important things in life – love, joy, laughter, wonder, the soaring spirit. And you cannot put them in a test tube!

For these and other reasons, there has been a revolution against the cold grey world of Enlightenment physics, chemistry and regimentation. These days we celebrate the spiritual sides of our nature which have been too long neglected. And we are right to do so!

Your second important insight, Melanie, is your impression that the church knows little about spirituality like this. It is a fair criticism. After all, when did you last laugh in church? When did you see love flowing among the congregation? When were the worshippers last lost in wonder, love and praise of the God they were supposed to be celebrating? Is a church service not always run from the front? And usually by some sort of professional? Don't the people have only a minimal part to play? They may not even get a word of welcome as they come in. In many churches the prayers are read out of a book by a man wearing strange clothes and using antiquated language. The hymn tunes are dreary and quite out of touch with modern music. And in real life nobody speaks uninterrupted for quarter of an hour. After the service ends, there is sometimes not even a cup of coffee: the congregation seem thankful to go home! To be sure, that is a worst case scenario, but there are many places where it is still rather like this, and more importantly it is the impression that lasts with so many people who have been forced to go to church as children, and escaped as soon as they could. So, Melanie, I cannot quarrel with your impression about some unspiritual churches. But may I make a suggestion? There is sure to be a church near you – and near most of us – that is full of joy, that is growing, that appeals to all types and all ages, and that really nourishes the spirit. It might be worthwhile seeking out one of these. They are, I am glad to say, on the increase.

But there are one or two points I would like to put to you and those who share your outlook. The first is that the spirituality you so obviously appreciate is indeed bigger than the church. But that does not necessarily mean that all of it is right or healthy! For example, you say you believe in ghosts, but there is nothing like the evidence for ghosts that there is for Jesus – hard evidence that it is impossible to doubt. You believe in horoscopes, and read yours daily. That suggests that the stars determine our lives. Such a view is the very opposite of spiritual and liberated: it means that we are in bondage to cold forces which we can do nothing to change. People in the ancient world who had no understanding of a living God tended to believe in one of two impersonal forces: luck or the stars. Everything in life was either a lottery or else predetermined. A great fourth-century thinker who later became a Christian, Augustine of Hippo, used to believe that the stars controlled everything – until he noticed that people born on the same day under the same star had totally different lives. Then he realized how foolish it was.

I mention these two topics, Melanie, from your own words, because they illustrate how wildly spirituality can lead us astray. There has to be some boundary to authentic spirituality. And this is what the Christian gospel offers us. Not the 'rites and rituals that kill off spirituality' which you rightly reject, but the guidelines of the God who made us and who loves us. No insubstantial ghost, but the God who came among us to show us what he is like. No cold determinism from the stars but the freedom of knowing and loving him, and sharing our lives with him. That is how the spiritual side of our nature finds fullest expression. What's the point of resting in some created object when you can know the Creator? What's the point of trying to quench your thirst elsewhere when you can drink the cool, refreshing water of a real relationship with the God who made you?

I am reminded of some words in the Bible spoken by the prophet Jeremiah long ago:

> Be appalled, O heavens, at this,
>   be shocked, be utterly desolate,
>   says the LORD,
> for my people have committed two evils:
>   they have forsaken me,
> the fountain of living water,
>   and dug out cisterns for themselves,

cracked cisterns
　　that can hold no water.

(Jeremiah 2:12–13)

Not quite how we would describe it, with all our mod cons. But the point is clear enough. We have turned our back on God. We prioritize our pleasures, our relationships, our finances – and find they do not satisfy. And my experience, and that of millions, Melanie, is that when we change direction, and start bringing God back into the picture, we can, as you rightly say, 'talk, pray to him at any time'. Indeed, we will find, as you dare to hope, 'that he is always there for you, and overlooking you'. True, 'you can't do the gardening in the church'. But you can talk to God as you do the gardening. I often do!

2. 'THE CHURCH IS JUST TOO INFLEXIBLE'

Annette is in her early 40s. She's got three children, four dogs, two rabbits, and works in a beauty parlour. She likes to work out but doesn't have as much chance to as she would like, since her children enjoy rugby, swimming, brownies and scouts, and she 'has a second job as a taxi service'.

She has had very little experience of church: some half-hearted and rather uninspiring experiences during childhood and since then just christenings, funerals, weddings (including her own) and the occasional Christmas service.

Her big problem with the church is that it is too inflexible. She had to jump through various hoops in order to get married in church and didn't bother getting her children christened subsequently.

'It's the inflexibility of them,' she says. 'You know, even when you go and seek them out, and even if you only want a part of their lifestyle or a part of their beliefs, they are not willing. They want you to have the whole package. And not all of us need that in our lives . . . instead of you being able to dip in/dip out. They are not that flexible, I feel.'

As far as Annette is concerned, it is all or nothing when it comes to religion, and she isn't interested in the all. She doesn't agree with everything that she thinks the church believes and, therefore, as far as she is concerned, she is out of the fold.

In any case, she feels quite strongly about what she considers to be the church's responsibility to society and its refusal to fulfil it. 'The church should reflect what we want,' she says at one point. 'The church should not dictate to us that you can get married, you can't get married. We want to get married. We are consumers of the church.'

She hasn't vowed never to set foot in a church again – she admits to quite liking Christmas carol services – but she has no intention of turning to the church for spiritual help. The inflexibility she feels she has experienced does not fit in with her lifestyle or with her image of what the church should be.

Response

Since Annette is in her early 40s, her childhood churchgoing days would have been some thirty years ago. And in those days the church, particularly the Church of England, could fairly be described as inflexible. There was one set service for morning, evening and Holy Communion – and it was all out of a book written three hundred years earlier. So the language was beautiful but so antique that you would need a dictionary to understand it. The clergy used robes that were very alien to where most people were coming from. Remarriage in church was not allowed, but even in those days there was the opportunity to have a service of thanksgiving in church after remarriage in a Registry Office. And everyone had the right to be baptized, married and buried in the parish in which they lived, or in another parish if they were on the electoral roll. So maybe it was not so ungenerous after all! But I grant your main point, Annette. The church was pretty inflexible. And that is a legitimate turn-off.

However, if you were to dip your toes into the church these days, I think you would find it very different. Many people don't go near it, because they have been so fed up with what they were taken to as a child. But if you did, I think you would find great variety. You see, society has changed enormously in the last thirty-five years. It is, as you point out, the age of consumerism, the age of choice. And at least the liveliest churches have recognized that fact. You see, the church is not meant to be a building or a hierarchy or an institution, but what the New Testament calls the body of Christ. That means it is supposed to be something like the visible expression of Jesus. And when Jesus was on earth he did not isolate himself in a building or stand on his dignity. He mixed naturally with people, speaking not in Elizabethan English but in the common language that was easily under-stood, using vivid and memorable stories, healing people who were ill, and in short being such an attractive person that people went into voluntary unemployment for a few days in order to hang out with him.

Well, the church in recent years has been taking a leaf out of his book. In matters of dress, for example, many churches have jettisoned robes in favour of ordinary clothes. The music has changed drastically: there is a mass of modern songs to express today's worship, alongside the best of the traditional hymns. Many churches find even the modern revised services too stuck-in-the-mud, and operate on a diet of worship, testimony, Scripture, teaching (often with visual aids and Powerpoint presentations), prayer, and an exten-sive time of fellowship over coffee and something to eat afterwards. You are not burdened with three or four books as you go in: everything appears by computer-generated projection. Sunday is not the only worship occasion. Often mid-week evening gatherings take its place as people find their lives so crowded that the weekends are the only chance for some down time with the family in a heavily pressurized working week.

But that is only the tip of the iceberg. Churches now take all sorts of forms. Almost everyone has heard of the Alpha course. Its meals, its openness to questions of any kind, its clear presentations, and its friendliness are highly attractive.

So is the opportunity to experience God's reality on the day away which features in all the Alpha courses. Well, is it surprising that many of these groups gain so much from the ten weeks or so together that they do not want to split up? Some of them develop into churches of their own. And the whole process is aided by the growth of what are known as cell churches.

Worldwide, these cell churches are the fastest and most relational way to live out the Christian faith, which, by the way, is growing faster than at any time in history. Now they never tell you that on the media, do they? But it's true. Cell churches represent a 'two-winged' approach to being the church that stresses both the small and the large expressions of Christian community (the cell and the celebration). People often come together for a large 'celebration' full of life and joy on Sundays, but the cell lies at the heart of the movement. Normally the cell contains a dozen or so members. They meet in someone's home. The welcome is extensive and draws everyone in. The leaders are ordinary people, not clergy. There are four main functions in a cell meeting – worship, a short talk from the Bible (or perhaps the application of what was taught in the celebration the previous Sunday), personal care, and an outward orientation. Everyone is actively involved in the cell. Personal needs are usually met as each individual receives care and prayer during a time of ministry. Everyone in the cell is involved in inviting others to come and join them. Yes, and other people come! They are amazed by the warmth, relevance and life of the cell. The cell expands – and then splits into two, and the process takes off again.

Some may feel cell churches sound a bit too intense, but there are lots of other models. I celebrated Christmas one year in a fish and chip shop that the local church had recently taken over. The men had painted the walls. The counter remained as something to lean on and put food and drink on. There were no seats – they had not got round to that yet. Everyone on the small estate had been personally invited, and loads of them came – with their babies, their kids, their Christmas presents and their dogs. It was a wonderful time of worship, joy, laughter and food, and a lot more like the original Christmas than some lofty cathedral worship – though there is a place for that too.

The small town of Bracknell in Berkshire offers another model. Mark Meardon and three musical friends in their twenties took over a small youth service in town, called 'Eternity'. It had been planned by adults, but Mark changed all that. In January 1995, and with a budget of £20, they set out to establish a community where young people could help plan the service and could experience God's love for themselves. Before long 'Eternity' had grown to 150, with a core of young people meeting mid-week for Bible study, companionship and prayer in small groups for their friends.

They started a drop-in café, 'Evoke', in 1997, a low-key place to chill out, and they met on a Friday evening. But a year or so later the numbers began to drop. The youth culture was moving away from the café to the dance floor. So they kept the principle behind 'Evoke' – to be a relaxed place where Christians and non-believers could meet and chat. But they allowed 'Evoke' to die. In its place 'Eclipse' was born, complete with dance, live DJs, Playstation and a non-alcoholic bar. And guess what? A hundred per cent of the youth in the town have made some contact with 'Eternity' and its successors, and a quarter of them enter into an active contact with a church. Nobody could call that stuffy and inflexible, could they?

I have mentioned cafés as venues for churches. 'Rubik's

Café' in Bristol runs twice a month on a Saturday night and is a magnet in the area. People who never went to church go there and are gradually being drawn into the faith. Their other venture is 'Rubik's Cube', held every Monday, and it is designed to speak to the bar crowd, through music, food and drink, and friendships. It is not only drawing people to Christ, but was rated recently in a national DJ magazine as being 'on the cutting edge of the drum and bass scene'.

There are quite a lot of modern expressions of the church like this around the country, Annette. Might be worth looking into one in your area. I don't think you would be able to maintain that the church is so inflexible. You might just find it the most exciting thing in your life, and that of your family.

There were a couple of other things I noticed in your comments. First, you feared that because you could not buy into all the church's beliefs you would be 'out of the fold'. It is not like that, Annette. You don't have to believe anything before you start. Most people these days find a satisfying faith through belonging to a lively Christian community before they believe much at all. Don't for heaven's sake think it is all or nothing, or there would not be room for any of us in the church!

The other thing is this. You made a very interesting statement. You reckoned that 'the church should reflect what we want . . . we are consumers of the church'. Sounds good but it won't really work. We are indeed consumers in shops and we pick and choose. But we would not think of ourselves as consumers in a family situation or even a well-run business. Well, the church is the community of Jesus, his extended family if you like. It tries to march to his drum and go his way – it is not there just to give us what we want, but to liberate us from our self-centredness and make us a bit more like our leader, Jesus. So, unlike the supermarket, the church is not something where we are just consumers. We are called to be disciples, or 'learners' and to get stuck in to this family of his, with its need for give and take, or we will never discover the joy of authentic Christian spirituality for ourselves.

3. 'CHRISTIANS ARE SUCH HYPOCRITES'

George is in his early 60s, married, with three children and seven grandchildren. He retired from the Civil Service a few years ago but works part-time as a delivery driver now, in order to 'earn some spare cash and get out of the house'.

Neither he, his wife, nor his children are religious, and George is quite proud of that fact. He is quick to defend his moral credentials and is profoundly irritated at the suggestion that he is a less moral person for not being religious.

'I've got high morals but I would never say I was religious,' he says. 'I feel as though I've got morals. You know I'd never do anything to hurt anybody . . . whereas sometimes if you meet some people who are very religious, they sort of shove it down your throat.'

George's own family background was strictly religious, with both parents attending their local Anglican church twice on a Sunday when he was a boy. He grew up in the church family and was on familiar terms with the various vicars and curates who came to tea. Consequently, he had a good idea of what was going on behind closed doors, and as he got older, became less and less impressed with the difference between what he saw and heard in church on a Sunday and what he knew was going on in the parish.

George is also adamant, however, that he is a Christian, writing 'Christian' on the various forms he is required to fill in (including the National Census). He justifies this by explaining that there are two kinds of Christian, those who live decent, moral lives and those who go to church and make a big fuss of it. This latter group are, he insists, hypocrites.

'It's a kind of paradox . . . between saying they are Christian

and [what they do] . . . you know, superficially they do all the things that Christians should do, but . . . the way they treat others and behave and respond to crises, that actually is not very Christian'. 'Christianity sometimes kind of cloaks itself,' he continues, '[Christians] like to think of themselves as Christian but in my understanding of the word they are not.'

Having worked hard all his life and done his utmost to treat people fairly without ever boasting about it, he feels very strongly about this hypocrisy of those who (he thinks) like to proclaim their morality.

'My choice is that the church doesn't come into it,' he says. 'I just live my life as I believe I should live it, and make my decisions and hope they are good ones . . . I don't have to go round pretending that I am going to be holy as long as I'm good and . . . basically look after . . . my family'.

Response

Well, George, there are a few confusions here! So why don't we try to clear those up first, and then have a look at your main conviction, that Christians are hypocrites?

The first confusion comes from thinking that Christianity is the same as being moral. It isn't! If it was, it would be called Morality not Christianity! Some of the most moral people who have ever existed have not been Christians. Think of Socrates and Plato in the ancient world, or many Buddhists or Muslims today, who have a very high moral code. To be sure, Christians have high moral standards too: they try to derive them from Jesus, who on any showing lived a perfect life. But Christians are not so foolish or narrow-minded as to suppose that only they do good things and live a kind, unselfish life. What's more, they try to be quick to recognize their failures: that is why repentance or apology to God figures so prominently in Christian worship. No, a Christian is a 'Christ's man'. That's what the word means. A Christian has a personal relationship with Jesus: that's the Christian's defining characteristic. And he or she tries hard not just to keep commonly accepted standards, but to please Jesus Christ. We don't always succeed, as you have perceived.

The second confusion is that there are two sorts of Christians. There are those like you who don't believe in Jesus and don't go to church, but write 'Christian' on their census form. Then there's the other lot that are religious. Two different groups under the same name? Hardly. The first Christians did not call themselves by that name at all. They called themselves 'disciples' or learners. They knew they had not arrived yet : they recognized that they were on a journey, or climbing a mountain. They had not got there yet, but they knew they had begun with Jesus. It was other people who called them Christians. Why? Because they behaved like Jesus, they spoke of Jesus, they sacrificed for Jesus, they loved Jesus. The New Testament could never countenance the idea that you could be a Christian without following Christ and being devoted to him. But as the centuries passed, Christianity became the main faith of Europe, and indeed much of the whole world, since no other faith has ever approached it in numbers. So people began to call countries Christian if they had a majority of Christians in them. It was a broad generalization: obviously not everybody in any country is a devoted follower of Jesus Christ, or ever has been. But because Christians tried to live loving, generous, sacrificial lives, the name had a good smell! And now in Britain where Christianity has shrunk a lot, the idea that a Christian life and a good life have a lot in common leads people to say that they are Christians, when what they really are claiming is that they live good lives. You know the saying 'I'm as good a Christian as those who go to church!' What it really means is that 'I live as good a life as those who go to church.' You may well do, George. But who says?

I am afraid there is a third confusion in what you said. I don't think you will thank me for pointing it out. You feel very strongly, don't you, about church people who go round proclaiming their morality (have you really met such people?). And you point out that you have always done your utmost to treat people fairly without boasting about it. But as I read what you have said, it seems to me that you are the one who is boasting, rather loudly. 'I've got high morals . . . I'd never do anything to hurt anybody . . . I live my life as I believe I should live it, and make my decisions and hope they are good ones. I'm good, and basically look after my family.' Now perhaps you made that claim without really thinking, but sometimes our real attitudes slip out unnoticed, do they not? I hear you saying you don't like Christians who proclaim their virtues. But are you not doing precisely the same thing?

However I do not want to evade your main challenge: that Christians are hypocrites. You insisted rather strongly that religious people who go to church and make a big fuss of it are hypocrites.

The word 'hypocrite' is an old Greek word. It means an actor. So the charge is that Christians are actors. They don't mean what they say. They are not real. I am ashamed to say that this is sometimes true. There are appalling scandals which from time to time hit the headlines in the papers. But it would be a mistake to start out with the idea that everyone who goes to church is a paid-up Christian. You will find people in Christian churches for all sorts of reasons. Some of them are seeking a meaning in life. Some of them are simply battered by what they have been through. Some of them are habitual churchgoers – they go to church as thoughtlessly as they put their clothes on in the morning. Some of them may not be real: like Judas among the disciples of Jesus. The Judas strain has remained in the Christian church. Jesus himself was very vocal against hypocrisy in his followers.[1] When you find Christians who are hypocrites, they are going dead against the teaching of Jesus. But I think you will find that as an overall description of Christians the charge of hypocrisy simply will not wash, and I will show you why.

Think of the first followers of Jesus, whom we read of in the New Testament. Most of them were killed beause they could not keep quiet about Jesus. The same thing happened to many of their successors once the Colosseum in Rome was built at the end of the first century, to men and women like Bishop Ignatius who was torn limb from limb by the lions. That strain of martyrs has continued throughout the history of the church. There have never been so many people killed for their loyalty to Jesus as in the past hundred years. Or think of the missionary movement in the nineteenth century. Men gladly went out to Nigeria with the gospel in the early days when the expectation of life was less than a year. And there were always those ready to step into the dead men's shoes. Think of the liberation of slaves, or the launching of Trades Unions, the passionate self-giving for the dying that we see in a Mother Teresa and her Sisters of Mercy, or for destitute children in people like Thomas Barnardo. Any suggestion of hypocrisy is ludicrous. These people were real, so real that they did not count their lives as precious to themselves but were prepared to give them up for the cause of Christ. Think of the politicians, the educators, the artists, the poets and musicians who have been inspired by Jesus of Nazareth, have used their gifts in his service and have remained loyal to him until their dying day. There have been many blemishes in the church's record, but there is no faith, no ideology, that has had such a distinguished record of public service, social and moral advance and self-sacrifice as the Christians'. If you removed all the Christians from Britain's voluntary services they would completely collapse.

Yes, a few of our churchpeople may be play actors. This was probably much more true in the Victorian days, when it was fashionable to go to public worship, than now. Some undoubtedly went because it was the done thing, but remained strangers to Jesus Christ, and did not allow their churchgoing on Sunday to affect the way they behaved from Monday to Saturday. That is the shame of the church. We acknowledge it. But George, spare a thought for the value of the church, when it has been truly committed to Jesus, and consequently has reflected his life and his love to a needy world. I understand how you feel. You used to go to church as a youngster and saw things there that turned you off and made you cynical about Christianity. Understandable. But George, take a second look. A look at what has been achieved by genuine Christians. And a look at Jesus himself. You may be disappointed by the failures of his followers. But you will never have cause to be disappointed with him.

A final word, George. You seem very confident of being so moral and so good. It might be worth remembering that when people flattered Jesus and called him good he questioned it. 'Why do you call me good?' he asked. 'There is nobody good except God' (Matthew 19:17; Mark 10:18; Luke 18:19). As St Paul put it a few years later, 'There is no-one who is righteous, not even one; . . . no-one seeks

God . . . there is no distinction, since all have sinned and fall short of the glory of God' (Romans 3:11, 22–23). That is true of everyone, George, including you. And that is why we all need a rescuer, a saviour, if we are ever to get through to God. Mercifully, God has provided one.

4. 'RELIGIOUS PEOPLE ARE TOO INTOLERANT'

'For about five years I have looked for spiritual direction. My inquisitiveness and my search still goes on but I am not hell-bent on trying to find answers. I am just waiting.' So says Helen, mother of two late-teenagers, part-time librarian, and self-confessed spiritual traveller.

Having put much of her life 'on hold' whilst bringing up the children, Helen is using her new found spare time to explore life to the full. She and her husband have started to holiday in new resorts, eat at new restaurants and explore new avenues in life.

One of these 'avenues' is spirituality. Helen isn't quite sure what that means, but she feels sure that there is more to life than 'materialism' and 'consumerism'. To date, her spiritual search has not provided her with any answers, but, as she indicates, she is quite happy to be inquisitive and just wait.

Helen is interested in a number of spiritual paths, but she has no time for Christianity, or any another organized religion. The church, she reckons, is obsessed with rules and regulations, and dangerously intolerant.

'One thing I am absolutely sure about is that I could not and would not want to embrace the church,' she says. 'Its narrowness. I think it is very bigoted. I don't think the church is willing to look at very important grey areas in life. I don't think it is truly willing to look at the very painful areas like homosexuality.'

When pressed, she is unable to think of examples other than that of homosexuality, but that does not change her point of view. Religion, Helen says, is about control, whereas spirituality is about freedom. It is narrow-minded, whereas spirituality is open. Above all, religion is intolerant, whereas spirituality is about tolerance.

Intolerance is, as far as Helen is concerned, the root of the world's problems, and religion (as opposed to spirituality) is at the root of most of this intolerance. 'If religious groups could respect each other's individual opinion . . . that would be really good, you know,' she says.

As far as she is concerned, religion and religious intolerance (she uses the terms almost synonymously) are at the heart of most of the world's trouble spots: Indonesia, Nigeria, Israel, Kashmir, 9/11. She doesn't quite claim that a world without religion would be a world without trouble, but she does think that religion justifies far too much intolerant small-mindedness, which itself breeds wars, terrorism and atrocities.

She does not necessarily think Christianity is any worse than any other religion – she has a few choice words for Islam! – but she admits to not knowing enough about other faiths to comment on them. Christianity, she says, is bad enough.

Her opinions have had little impact on her spiritual search – she remains keen on exploring the spiritual world – but they have had a profound impact on the way she is searching. If the avenue has a hint of organized or institutionalized religion about it, she is not interested.

Response

Thank you so much for these comments, Helen. A great many modern people feel that way. You realize that there is more to life than materialism and consumerism. You know that life gets blighted when we simply live for ourselves, for money and what money can buy. And that is a vital discovery. I know someone who asked, 'What will it profit them to gain the whole world and forfeit their life?' (Mark 8:36). We can't get far without money, but money is a root cause of all kinds of evil, and to live for it is a destructive delusion. It is fascinating how many rich people go on record about how unhappy they are!

I am delighted that you have turned your back on consumerism and embarked on the spiritual search. That is very up to date, but it leads people to a whole variety of destinations: channelling, crystals, cults, oriental religions, tantric sex and bike rides to watch the sun go down over the sea. You are savouring a new freedom after looking after your kids for many years, and that freedom is immensely important to you – and indeed to all of us.

Your search for spirituality has led you to make some enquiries into organized religion. You have found it wanting, and who can blame you? The average church or synagogue is not the most exciting place you can imagine. It does not shout to you about freedom!

The very word 'organized' is something that sticks in the throat of true freedom. Quite rightly you do not want to be told when to worship, when to stand up and sit down or kneel. Such organization is the very antithesis of freedom, and unfortunately it marks most religious groups, as you have noticed. Of course you would be the first to admit that organization, however light, is a necessary part of life. We could not have absolute freedom to drive on whichever side of the road we wanted. We need some organization to run a home, an office or a country properly. You must have had some organization in your home while bringing up the kids, even though they are now teenagers and no doubt react against the 'house rules'. No, it is not so much organization that is the trouble, but when organization crowds out life and inhibits personal growth and discovery. That's when it becomes a real pain. And you are right to say so.

I was intrigued by what you have to say about the love of the search. You remind me of a mantra that used to be chanted in the days of my youth, 'To travel is better than to arrive.' That was said by religious people, actually, Helen. Like you, they were impatient of the control their religious observance seemed to impose. Like you, they revelled in the freedom of travel rather than in the arrogant certainty of those who think they have arrived. And yet we do want to arrive. You are content to wait, you say. But you are waiting for something that really satisfies your love of freedom, are you not? Surely you don't want to spend your one precious life being perpetually uncommitted, do you? G. K. Chesterton once said, a little unkindly, of H. G. Wells, 'He thinks that the opening of the mind is simply the opening of the mind; whereas I am incurably convinced that the object of opening the mind, as of opening the mouth, is to shut it again on something solid.'

There's another thing we need to look at in what you say: tolerance. These days intolerance is the ultimate no-no. Tolerance is the supreme virtue. And this is a comparatively recent development. The fact is that once the majority of virtues go down the tube, tolerance is the only one left. And it had better be, or you will get a very bumpy ride through life. But it is interesting that in the New Testament you never find tolerance put forward as a virtue. You have a lot of other virtues stressed like gentleness, goodness, courage, unselfishness and so on. But at the top of the tree is not tolerance but love. Tolerance is a negative putting up with other people. Love is a positive putting ourselves out for them. There's a world of difference between the two. And when you stop to think about it, an all-embracing tolerance is not so impressive. Are judges to tolerate gangsters? Should we let paedophiles out among schoolchildren in the name of tolerance? Are all fouls on the football field OK if you have got a nice tolerant referee? The idea is ridiculous. It sounds good but we frankly don't believe it, nor can we live with it. Societies, games, religious organizations have norms of expected behaviour, house rules if you like. And if you join that society or sport or religion, you are expected to abide by them.

Of course that does not mean that religious organizations should be intolerant and unloving towards one another. That used sometimes to be the case. The sparks used to fly between different brands of Christians. But you don't find much of that these days. I would guess that I spend much more time among people of different faiths than you do, Helen, and I have noticed in recent decades something very important. We have learnt to respect one another even if we do not agree with one another. That really is vital. We inhabit a small planet and if the different religions and ideologies do not learn to live with mutual respect, the outlook is very bleak indeed. That is why extremists of any sort, particularly suicide bombers, are such a threat to world peace and stability. Jesus was full of courtesy and respect for all types of people – churchmen, prostitutes, peasants, Roman soldiers, and so on, though he did not always agree with them. His followers must be the same. When they don't, they betray their Master. He told his close followers not to moan about others who saw their discipleship in a somewhat different light.[1] Most of all, he forbade the use of violence, even when one of his followers drew a sword to try to save him from arrest.[2] 'Turn the other cheek' was his teaching – and his practice.

But Helen, your main point is a very important one. You seem to be convinced that if you have organized religion it must mean control. Once again I have some sympathy with you. The word 'religion' comes from the Latin, and it means something that binds or ties. The idea seems to have originated with a pact, an agreement between Numa, the first king of Rome, and Jupiter, king of the gods. It was a sort of 'You scratch my back, I'll scratch yours' arrangement. Numa would ensure that the smell of sacrifices always rose up to delight Jupiter's nostrils. Jupiter, for his part, would ensure that the Roman armies always carried the day. And most religions are like that. They depend on rules which benefit both parties. But real Christianity is not like that. That is why I rather dislike calling Christianity a religion. It is essentially a relationship of love between an incredibly generous God and his grateful followers. And it is not about control but about freewill and generosity on both sides.

Think of Jesus for a moment. He was the most liberated person that ever lived. He refused to be bound by the rules of the Jewish religion. You would find him scandalizing the religious by healing someone on a Sabbath day.[3] You would find him eating food that the Jews thought ceremonially unclean.[4] He refused to tolerate the corruption that went on in temple commerce, but threw the money changers out of the temple.[5] He freely chose to go to Jerusalem knowing he was walking to his death.[6] If you read the story of Jesus on trial before Pilate, it is very obvious who is the free man and who is the craven coward.[7] There was never man more free than Jesus of Nazareth. And his followers need to be like him. Often they are not, as you rightly point out. That is a very black mark against the Christian community. It is all too easy to allow our liberty as followers of the Great Lover to degenerate into legalism. It is plain to behold in many a church. But not all. My observation is that there is a large proportion, perhaps a majority, of churches where relationship, not coercion, is the order of the day.

These are the churches that are true to the nature of Jesus. After all, what does he offer people? He is Christ the

Liberator, and he offers release from guilt through free forgiveness when we do not deserve it one little bit. He offers freedom from habits which have chained us for many years, because his Spirit comes to live inside us and break their power. He sets people free from the fear. Our society is riddled with fear. Fear of terrorism, fear of what others think, fear that our good looks will fade, fear that the job will fold up, fear of death. Jesus liberates people from fear. His follower Simon Peter came to realize that. 'Cast all your anxiety on him,' he advised 'because he cares for you' (1 Peter 5:7). Many people are enslaved by loneliness. Here again Jesus sets us free. He promises that he will be with us always, and that nothing in all the world can separate us from his love.[8] And one thing more. Jesus sets people free from aimlessness. So many go through life without any overall aim: just to get through the day, or survive the week, or to get married, to have kids, to retire with a pension that has not shrunk too much.

But once you get gripped with the truth that Jesus is alive, he is risen from the dead, he is with you always – you have something to live for! It gives a new zest and purpose to living. It is true spirituality, Helen, not religious control. Jesus never forces his followers to do what he wants. He asks them, and they are free to say yes or not. A wise man long ago said 'Love God and do what you want'. It makes sense, actually, although it sounds risky, because if we do love him we will want to please him. Seeking to please Jesus Christ lies at the heart of Christian freedom. It is the true lover's response.

5. 'YOU CAN'T TRUST WHAT IS IN THE BIBLE'

Adam is 24 and has been working for a local council in South London for nearly three years. He is thinking of moving on. He is single and 'between girlfriends'. He plays football for his local team but is consistently disappointed by their performance.

He has no religious faith at all, although his upbringing was 'quite Christian'. Both his parents attended church irregularly when he was young, and he and his younger brother were 'dragged along', at first willingly but latterly against their will. There were better things to be doing, like playing football, on a Sunday morning.

Fifteen or so years of reasonably regular church attendance has given him a rudimentary understanding of the Christian faith, and in a group interview with half a dozen peers, he is often able to correct them and lead the discussion when it comes to factual issues.

His basic objection to Christianity is that it simply isn't true. He is agnostic about the existence of God, but quite certain that what is written in the Bible, which he recognizes as the foundation stone of Christianity, is not reliable.

'The Bible contradicts itself,' he says. '[There are] stories in the New Testament from Matthew, Mark, Luke and John . . . that's four different people, and there are [often] four different stories as well'.

The reason for this, he explains, is that 'the Gospels weren't written at the time of Jesus . . . [but] several years afterwards . . . they were written at a certain time but well after Jesus died so the fact that they were written after he died would lend itself to the belief that the stories were exaggerated'.

In addition to this, as far as Adam is concerned, historical records dating from so long ago are by their very nature untrustworthy. 'Back then there wasn't such a thing as the media, so knowledge wasn't as widespread, like people didn't know as much.' The idea of information being passed by word of mouth is proof of unreliability as far as he is concerned.

Not only are the Gospels contradictory, but individual stories do not hold water, either. 'If you pull the Bible to pieces,' he continues, 'it's full of contradictions. . . . For example Adam and Eve had two sons . . . how did the world go on?'

As if this weren't enough, the Bible contradicts itself morally as well as historically. 'You go through the Bible,' he says, 'and all the commandments are broken. So it's like, OK . . . you've got to do the Ten Commandments, but literally every one is broken isn't it. So [that's] a huge contradiction.'

The result of all this is that he has no interest in religion or Christianity. What's more, he is quite contemptuous of Christians who do not exercise the same scepticism over the Bible as he does. 'They read it and they don't question it, that's what I don't get, because, me, I would question it.'

Response

This is an important question, Adam. I am glad you have raised it so sharply. I am particularly glad to read your final complaint: 'They read it and they don't question it, that's what I don't get, because, me, I would question it.' Quite right. You should question it.

You see, the Bible is the record which claims to give us the most staggering story in the world: that there is a living God who cares for us so much that he has made himself known to us. This record came to us first through the limited understanding of the Old Testament characters and prophets. But the climax and core of this record is when Jesus was born into this world. He claimed to reveal to us what God is like. The whole New Testament, that is, the second half of the Bible, is concerned with the coming, the teaching and healings, the death and resurrection of Jesus – together with his massive claims. Those who had been his friends and followers give considerable testimony to the truth about Jesus. A lot of their testimony is incidental, written in letters they sent to the earliest churches of believers. That actually makes it the more impressive – they were not trying to prove a point. But they were trying to draw others into the rich companionship with Jesus, victor over death, that they enjoyed. This is how one of them, a close companion of Jesus, ends his account: 'Now Jesus did many other signs in the presence of his disciples, which are not written in this book. But these are written so that you may come to believe that Jesus is the Messiah, the Son of God, and that through believing you may have life in his name' (John 20:30–31).

John, who wrote this, had followed Jesus closely for three years. Orthodox Jew though he was, he had gradually become convinced that this Jesus was no mere man, but that he embodied all that could be known of God in human flesh and blood. This was the most important discovery of his life. So he was passionate to share it with others, not only during the rest of his long life, but long after he was dead, through the book that he had written. In it he gives seven great signs that show Jesus was more than human: he brought God into our scene. Then there was the greatest sign of all, the cross and resurrection. John tells us all about this. He tells us of an agnostic like Thomas (perhaps a little bit like you?) falling down at the feet of the risen Jesus, convinced at last that he really was the conqueror of death. And John then comes out with the passage I have quoted. He wants everyone critically to examine the evidence he has given about who Jesus really is. He wants them to go further, as he had done, once he was convinced by the evidence: to commit themselves to Jesus, and to discover to their amazement a whole new dimension of life. That is why John wrote his Gospel. He had found treasure, and he was determined to share it as widely as he could. In the centuries that followed it has led literally millions to belief in Jesus.

All down the years from then until now people have risked exposing themselves to the evidence in that book of John's. They have read it with an open mind. They have tried to find alternative explanations for the marvellous acts and words contained in it. But they have mostly failed, and come to the same conclusion as John the author, that this Jesus really did these things, really did die for us, really did rise from the chill of the grave, and can be encountered by anyone who is humble enough to ask.

Many a time I have been talking to an atheist, and suggested to him that there is a way by which he can be virtually certain whether or not the Christian story is true. I say, 'Why don't you read this Gospel with an open mind?' He will probably tell me that he did that as a kid when bits of it were rammed down his throat in RE lessons or Sunday school. But I say, 'No, I suggest you read it in a different way, perhaps at a sitting. Let the story sweep over you. See what you make of it. And as you do so, ask God to show you what truth there is in it.' 'I can't pray,' he will say: 'I am an atheist.' I reply, 'Well, here's a prayer you can use however atheistic you are. "God, I don't believe you exist, but I don't know everything. I might be wrong. So if you do exist, please show me what is true in this stuff and I will follow that truth wherever it leads, – even if it is to becoming a Christian."' Of course, if there is no God, that tentative prayer will mean nothing. But in reading the Gospel, you will have absorbed one of the most beautiful and influential books the world has ever seen. And that can't be bad, Adam – it's a great way to pass the time between girlfriends! But be careful. Almost every one to whom I have suggested that way of approach has become convinced that Jesus is real, and has become a follower of his. It's all about having an open mind, and letting the original evidence impact you.

That seems to me the most important issue you have raised, Adam, but there were several more.

You are worried that there are four different accounts of Jesus in the New Testament, four Gospels as we call them. They have an enormous amount in common. But on quite a lot of points they differ. Of course. No four people talking about their friend will ever say precisely the same things about him. They will all have the special emphasis their authors want to make. The Gospels are portraits of Jesus from different angles, painted by different people. They are not word for word the same. I should be very suspicious if they were. So would you if the *Sun*, *The Times*, the *Guardian* and the *Mirror* reported the same football match in exactly the same words. They all give their own interpretation of the game. But that enriches our understanding and does not diminish it. It is like that with the Gospels. They each have a different slant, but they all present us with the same figure, towering over the merely human, full of vitality, insight, truth and love.

You have another objection. The stories in the Gospels were not written down at the time but afterwards, and that could have opened the door for exaggeration and error.

Well, in the days after Jesus rose from the grave at the first Easter and sent them out to spread the gospel throughout the known world, the early followers of Jesus were too busy

preaching the good news of forgiveness, and new life both
now and after death, to sit down writing books. But before
long they did, as some of the eyewitness generation began
to die off. Nobody is quite sure when the Gospels were
written (certainly within 50 years of the death of Jesus), but
a lot of the sayings of Jesus seem to have been taken down
in shorthand during his lifetime. There were several forms
of shorthand in existence at that time. Moreover, the stories
would have been repeated time and again in a fairly fixed
way as the preachers told them. As a matter of fact, both
in Jewish and early Christian circles written testimony was
not valued nearly as highly as living tradition. In due course
these stories were written down, within the lifetime of those
who had heard Jesus. If they had cheated, and made up the
stories, they would have been shown up and laughed out of
court, and the young Christian movement would have been
finished. But nobody could rebut the main evidence that
they recorded.

I don't think we need spend time over an old chestnut like
the children of Adam and Eve. That story may well not be
intended to be taken literally but rather as a graphic picture
of our creation, our dependence on God, our failure, and the
first hints of God's rescue. If it is to be taken literally, then
there would have been marriages among the other children
of Adam and Eve – not a good move now, but inevitable
under those circumstances!

But before you dismiss Adam and Eve too readily, had
you noticed that some of the experts on the human genome
project are coming to the conclusion that the whole of
humankind is descended from one woman, whom the
scientists now call Eve? We can't be sure how many male
partners she may have had since this kind of genetic tracing
goes through the female line. But if all the different races did

originally spring from a single female – well, that's something to think about!

Nor need we spend time on the fact that God gives commandments and human beings fail to keep them. The Bible does not airbrush the nastiness out of life. It is shockingly honest about the failures of the men and women it speaks of. It is that very human failure which so called forth the love of God that he came among us to deal with the situation through the cross.

But, Adam, let me give you five good reasons for regarding the Bible very highly.

First, because it has been relentlessly attacked down the centuries, and in our own lifetime particularly ruthlessly in communist countries, and it not only survives but continues to be the world's bestseller.

Second, and much more importantly, because the greatest person who ever lived, Jesus Christ, gave the Scripture his unreserved support. He regarded it as inspired by God.[1] He saw it as utterly authoritative.[2] Time and again we find him saying 'The scriptures must be fulfilled' . When he says 'It is written', that is final.

The third important reason for taking Scripture very seriously indeed is the fact of its many prophecies which were fulfilled centuries later in the life and death of Jesus. Let us take five of them by way of illustration. Look up the whole of Isaiah 53, Micah 5:2, Jeremiah 23:5–6, Psalm 16:8–11. There you find predictions of a coming great ruler in Israel. We are told the place of his birth, the family from which he would come, his reception by the people, the fact and the details of his agonizing death and what it would achieve, the circumstances of his burial and his ultimate triumph. Those prophecies were precisely fulfilled in Jesus. There is no parallel to such fulfilment of prophecy anywhere in world literature. Isn't that very odd if the Bible is unreliable?

The fourth reason for giving great heed to Scripture is this. The Bible is not so much a book as a library. It was written over 1,500 years, in three languages, by an incredible variety of people. But you find one single picture of God – utterly loving, utterly holy and just, and the personal creative source of all life. You find one single picture of human beings – neither 'naked apes' nor 'little angels' but made in God's image and yet constantly going our own way and leaving him out: all the chaos in human affairs springs from that basic attitude of rebellion. And you find one single picture of divine rescue – he cares for us so much that he welcomes us back into his company, though it cost him death on the cross to make it possible. Now if you get ten people together in a room, you are likely to get ten different views of God, humans and salvation. Is it not remarkable that this book, the Bible, has such a unified view on these vital issues? Does it not suggest that behind the very varied human authors here was the all-shaping mind of God, longing to disclose himself to us?

And that leads me to my final conviction that the Bible really is God's message to us: experience. Once you start reading it, seeking to live it out, you become increasingly convinced of its truth, its wisdom and its power. Adam, you might be wise to give it a try!

6. 'SCIENCE HAS DISPROVED CHRISTIANITY'

Keith is married, in his late 40s and has two children. He works as an engineer and likes to think he has a clear, concise, rational mind. He is disdainful of the 'hocus-pocus' of spirituality and pseudo-scientific practices like alternative medicine. Religion falls safely into this category.

As far as he is concerned, the universe is an enormously complex but ultimately comprehensible and predictable machine, and the tool for understanding it is science. He illustrates this in a number of ways.

Generally speaking, science has proved itself much better at explaining the world than religion. 'We know how the world began and, you know, science questions all this theory about the creation theory and all these other things.' And this explanatory success is evident in virtually every aspect of modern life. 'With science you see a lot . . . you see the science of people having babies through IVF and things like that.'

More specifically, science has disproved a number of religious claims, creation being the most obvious one.

'Christians say that the world was made in six or seven days or something, and on the sixth day humans were made, but where in that six days were the dinosaurs made and when did they get wiped out? . . . It's like Darwin's theory of evolution . . . and the discovery of bacteria at the bottom of the sea and all that kind of stuff, millions and trillions of years old. That makes a lot more tangible sense to me, than this mythical God that is up there who is supposed to have single-handedly created the whole world, as is.'

Another example he cites is the Turin Shroud. 'You've got the Turin Shroud, haven't you, where scientists are now saying that

that couldn't possibly have been the robes that Jesus was buried with. So that is down to science again, isn't it?'

When pushed on these issues, particularly the issue of creation which in his mind is the most substantive disproof of Christianity, his reasoning becomes slightly more hesitant. He acknowledges, for example, that the world does seem to be shot through with signs of design, although he insists that is an optical illusion, in the same way as the sun appears to circle the earth. More chillingly, when pressed by another, more sceptical interviewee for proof of evolution, he says, slightly sheepishly, 'Even now you've got people who have got features that are more apelike than others, haven't you?'

He is also willing to recognize the comfort that believing in God may offer people, but he puts this down to wishful thinking. 'I don't [believe] because there's not enough scientific basis for it . . . it [would be] nice to believe that Santa exists too!'

Response

Keith, you may flatter yourself that you have 'a clear, concise, rational mind', but I am afraid you are not displaying it to best advantage in what you have to say on this subject.

Let's begin with your main point about creation. You will not find many Christians these days who believe that the world was made in six days, in the sense of 24-hour periods. For example, the seventh day is clearly not a matter of 24 hours but represents God's sabbath rest that still continues today. Moreover, in the Genesis account the differentiation of day from night does not come until the fourth 'day'[1]. So there weren't any days in your 24-hour sense until then! Neither Jewish rabbis nor early Christian fathers like Origen and Augustine imagined the world to be created in 7 periods of 24 hours each. There is a good reason for this. For frequently in the Bible the word 'day' is used of a long, unspecified period of time. Don't dismiss the biblical account because of a misunderstanding.

Keith, I want you to realize the Christian origins of science. Modern science was born in the sixteenth and seventeenth centuries in a Christian civilization, recently liberated from the shackles of religious authoritarianism by the Renaissance and the Reformation. It was pioneered by Christian men who saw God's works in nature and his words in Scripture as the twin facets of his self-disclosure. You seem to think that the universe is an enormously complex machine: well, few modern scientists would agree with you, but that was the view, broadly speaking, of Isaac Newton. He certainly did not see belief in God as incompatible with his model of the universe. He wrote his *Principia* in the assurance that 'this world could originate from nothing but the perfectly free will of God'. And Einstein, whose theory of relativity made a massive advance on Newton, was also a strong believer in God the Creator. Many of the founders of the Royal Society, scientists like Boyle, Ward and Barrow, saw no contradiction in directing their studies equally 'to the glory of God' and 'to the advantage of the human race'.

But you may say that even if science originated in Christian circles, a great divide has opened up between science and religion since Darwin's theory of evolution emerged. There is some truth in that. In the latter part of the nineteenth century there was a growing desire among English scientists to free themselves from church influence. They were not opposed to Christianity as such but rather to the control exercised by the Church of England. Science needed to assert its independence. That is the real reason why the partnership between Christianity and science which was strong in the early part of that century collapsed. In the first half of the nineteenth century, you found a country parson like Gilbert White pursuing his scientific studies in *The Natural History of Selbourne*, confident in his science and sure of his God. But later in that century, you encountered the famous and ill-natured debate between Thomas Huxley and the Bishop of Oxford about Darwinian evolution. Their positions were irreconcilable – and both thought they had won the argument!

To be sure, lots of people share your view, Keith, that Christianity has been disproved by science. That's almost a basic assumption for the person in the street, and it is supported by that crusader for atheism Richard Dawkins, who is always drawing a contrast between 'scientific proof' and the 'blind faith' of believers. This is a contrast that looks impressive but simply will not stand critical examination (see Alister McGrath's book, *The Twilight of Atheism*). The person who believes there is no God is just as much a man or woman of faith as the person who believes in God. They just believe different things, which neither can conclusively prove! What we need to examine is not belief but evidence. Evidence is the only solid ground on which belief should rest.

Science does not prove things. Scientists observe, and when they see a series of uniformities, they suggest a general law to account for them. They look for evidence to support or to counter this 'law' that they think they have found. But evidence is not absolute proof. It is capable of reassessment and modification. For centuries it had been regarded as self-evident, on universal evidence, that all swans are white – until Captain Cook found black swans in Australia! One contrary instance can cause scientists to revise their theories so as to include both the observed uniformities and the exception. Scientists call it 'radical theory change'. So if you imagine, Keith, that science has proved everything, and that it never changes its theories, you have another thing coming. The best scientists these days have a proper humility before the complexity of the world. They look for evidence of a general law, but they are open to evidence that causes them to rethink. That is precisely the way Christians operate, by the way. They look at the evidence for God's existence (see chapter 12), they examine the life and teaching of Jesus of Nazareth (see chapter 8), and they then decide whether that evidence warrants belief in God and commitment to Christ or not. Self-commitment on evidence. Scientists call it 'inference to the best explanation' but it is open to revision. Thoughtful Christians operate in just the same way.

The best scientific theories are not the narrowly detailed ones, but those that look for the big picture, and the explanation that makes most sense of it. And when you put together the evidence outlined in chapter 12, together with the fact that we can make moral judgments, relate to one another, appreciate beauty, and think – well, you can appreciate why many people reckon that the existence of God is the best explanation of the totality of our world and ourselves.

Let's pause on this thinking business for a moment. The fact that we can explain anything at all is remarkable: that by itself calls for explanation. 'God is revealed,' said the astronomer Kepler, 'both in the world and in the human mind reflecting on the world'. In other words, there is a resonance between our minds and the way the world is. How come? Is that compatibility between the mind and the external world an enormous fluke, or does it suggest that there is a living God who is both the source of our world and of the minds with which we seek to understand it. You might do well to read a top scientist, Professor John Polkinghorne. His books make much of this remarkable point.

The fact of the matter is, Keith, that the natural sciences neither prove nor disprove the reality of God. God is not small enough to be caught in the analytic net of the scientist. There is not just one way of knowing. The scientist who measures his material in the test tube and knows what he is doing, does not know his wife in the same way when he goes home. At least, he would be in deep trouble if he tried! There is the world of difference between what the philosophers call 'knowing by description' (the scientific way) and 'knowing by acquaintance' (the way we know friends – and God). But both are valid. Nor must we shrink God to cover the ever-decreasing gaps in our knowledge. The 'God of the gaps' is a pathetic travesty of the dynamic, infinite, all-pervasive God of the Bible, who is at the same time immanent within every aspect of his universe ('in him all things hold together', Colossians 1:17) and also immeasurably transcends our every conception ('he . . . dwells in unapproachable light', 1 Timothy 6:16).

You have to look at the evidence and see whether the atheist or the theist hypothesis makes the most sense. But let's have none of this rubbish about science killing off Christianity. Did you know that some 40% of active top-level scientists are Christians? They certainly don't believe your idea that science has disproved Christianity. Moreover, the late American evolutionary biologist, Stephen J. Gould, an open-minded agnostic who was one of the world's leading Darwinian scholars, wrote: 'To say it for all my colleagues for the umpteenth million time: Science simply cannot by its legitimate methods adjudicate the issue of God's possible superintendence of nature.' He continued,

'Either half of my colleagues are enormously stupid, or the science of Darwinism is entirely compatible with religious belief and equally compatible with atheism.'*

Interestingly enough, Charles Darwin himself contemplated ordination early on in his life, and carried belief in God into his studies in evolution. But his views on God became increasingly confused as he grew older, and he seems to have ended in agnosticism. But it was not because his evolutionary studies led him to deny the existence of God. The problem lay much closer to heart. He was deeply upset by the death of his daughter, his own father's agnosticism, and the consequences for his family in the light of the church's doctrine of hell. Darwin well understood that science itself is neutral. While he seems to have moved towards agnosticism, his close associate and fervent evolutionist Asa Grey remained a deeply committed Christian. As Nietzsche put it in another context, 'There are no facts: only interpretations'!

Once you are clear on this, Keith, your other problems may well fall into place. The earth may well be, as you say 'millions and trillions of years old'. Christians are totally open about its age. It makes not one iota of difference to our faith in an intelligent Force we call God behind whatever evolutionary or other processes brought the world to its present state. I hope you realize by now that the death of the dinosaurs is utterly irrelevant to the discussion. They were possibly, even probably, wiped out by the fouling of the atmosphere and the darkening of the sun after some massive

* I am indebted to my colleague Professor Alister McGrath (himself a distinguished scientist and theologian) for this quotation (Stephen J. Gould, *Scientific American* 267, 1992, pp. 118–121) as well as for some other insights in this chapter.

meteor hit the earth, and I am very happy to accept whatever date you like to give for this. It makes no difference to
Christian belief!

As for the Turin Shroud, if anything, that is one up for the
Roman Catholic Church! This remarkable object had been
a cause of controversy for many years, and in the interest
of clearing the matter up, the Church released part of the
shroud for scientific analysis, and accepted the result that
it was very unlikely to have been the garment in which the
body of Jesus was wrapped, since it apparently derived from
the Middle Ages. That is hardly a battle between religion and
science. Christians have no investment in believing that the
shroud is genuine. Our faith in Christ is not altered one way
or the other. And the Church did the right thing to encour-
age proper investigation – and then accepted the result.
Curiously enough, the issue of its genuineness is apparently not closed after all. Did you see the TV programme in
March 2004 showing that research suggests strongly that the
shroud is very probably after all a first-century AD product
from Palestine? I recently spent time in the research head-
quarters of the shroud, and there is now extensive evidence
that it is a first-century AD garment, and may well have
belonged to Jesus, though certainty is impossible.

You really are not doing yourself justice, Keith, if you try
to explain away the design which you recognize in nature as
an optical illusion. How would that work for the radar of a
bat, or the spawning habits of a salmon, travelling hundreds
of miles to the river where it was born in order to lay its
eggs? How could the direction-finding mechanism of newly
hatched young birds that migrate thousands of miles to a tiny
island in the midst of the Pacific that they have never seen,
be written off as an optical illusion? Since optics are what
you mention, how about the immensely intricate design in

the focusing equipment of your own eyes? To describe that as an optical illusion is utterly ridiculous. And to point to some of your fellow men as having ape-like faces is not only rude and probably racist; it fails to recognize the vast periods of time that need to have elapsed if evolutionary theory is true. Keith, you might do well to make less snap judgments and examine the evidence rather more closely.

7. 'THERE'S JUST TOO MUCH SUFFERING IN THE WORLD'

Morris is 41. He has one daughter, aged six. He is an open and positive individual with a particularly moving story.

'I got a huge amount of support from the church, because my wife was ill . . . she was quite Catholic, and she got a huge amount of support from the local Baptist church . . . She was ill for about two or three years, and when she died my daughter and I, we got a lot of support from them. It was just the support that I needed from fellow human beings. After the event, and continuing support. And a real community spirit you know, inviting us to their houses, bringing food to my house . . . it was totally genuine. When it's from the heart there's a difference. They didn't expect me to actually go to church, although I felt as though I should have gone and continued to go, but my beliefs had changed and I don't think they frowned upon that, you know. I could have continued, I could have perhaps converted in some way, but I didn't.'

Morris' story begins an interesting conversation in the group discussion in which he is a participant. Other respondents echo his sentiments, although without the same personal experience.

'Sometimes I think . . . it would be nice if God did exist,' one individual says, 'but then I think about, like, there's some really terrible things that happen in the world and I think, if there was a God, why are all those horrible things happening.'

This sentiment is refined by some other interviewees. 'It can't all have been good' one says. 'No, it can't be . . . We have to see suffering.' *Another makes the point that human beings themselves are responsible for much of the suffering in the world.*

'People dying hungry . . . that's probably because the governments aren't investing or the money is going elsewhere on arms.

So a lot of these disasters that we have, you know, man makes himself.'

Someone else points out that there is a certain hypocrisy in the way we blame God for bad things but don't thank him for good ones.

'You always seem to ask the question when things are going wrong for you – why me? But when things are going all right, you never seem to think, "Oh well, I'm the lucky one".'

Slowly, a consensus on this most complex, painful and personal of issues begins to appear in the group's discussion. God cannot be blamed for human wickedness, at least not directly, and suffering can, sometimes, bring about good. But, that said, God is responsible for natural disasters, except perhaps those which result from our abuse of the environment.

'If God created the world why does he allow things like earthquakes and famines and droughts and natural disasters to happen? Not man-made disasters, I mean, things like wars man creates for himself; but natural disasters, why does he allow them to happen?'

The concluding tone of the debate begun by Morris's story is one of resignation rather than of anger. God could have done a rather better job in creating the world, but as human beings we are not entirely free from blame.

Response

Suffering is a fact of life. We all have to face it, whatever our beliefs. Nobody has the luxury of being able to philosophize about it from an armchair. It will touch every one of us – mental, physical, emotional, and relational pain and suffering. It is part of our human condition. How are we going to make any sense out if it? How are we going to handle it when it comes along? That is the real issue.

Morris, you have handled your own suffering with great strength of character. Not a word of complaint against God when your wife died, but enormous appreciation of the support the local Baptist church has given you and your daughter, and not just a meal or two after the funeral, but continuing support, warm companionship. You realized that it was totally genuine. And when kindness like that comes from the heart, it makes an enormous difference. It nearly made you join them in that church – but not quite. Actually you almost feel a bit bad about that! That particular church gave an example of true Christian caring for a fellow human being without any strings attached, in the light of personal tragedy. It is very good to read what you said.

Your experience and willingness to talk about it clearly stimulated the group. Some were in agreement. Some were wistful, thinking how nice it would be if there was a God, but the problem of suffering was too damning on the other side. Some were honest enough to admit that we blame God when things go wrong, but don't come back and thank him when things go well. But the really interesting and unusual turn in the conversation came when some of the group got round to admitting that a great deal of the suffering in the world is man-made.

They really put their finger on it. The major cause of human suffering is the misuse of human freedom. One of the most precious attributes we have is our freedom. God cannot and will not take away our freedom when we use it against him. He will not intervene to stop train accidents when someone has forgotten to change the points, or to stop the plane being blown up when airport security has allowed a suicide bomber on board. The people in the group realized that the hunger in the world is due, not to the lack of food (there is plenty of food for everybody if only it was fairly distributed) but to selfishness, corruption and inefficiency in governments and protectionism by rich states. At present there are more than 30,000 children who die every day from preventable diseases because the rich countries simply do not care enough to help. The same applies to the wars, the thalidomide babies, the marriage breakdowns, and a whole mass of human suffering. It cannot be laid at God's door. It is our fault as human beings. And the group you talked it over with, Morris, admitted it.

Another important point that the discussion threw up was that suffering can sometimes produce good. Although God does not send suffering, he can and does use it. The pain and irritation in the oyster is what produces pearls. In human character qualities like courage, self-sacrifice and endurance can only come about in the face of suffering. Sometimes in my work I have found people becoming converted into integrated, joyful Christians after a death or some other disaster in the family. Sometimes the experience of acute suffering makes people intensely sensitive and compassionate to others in need. Sometimes the way a person handles suffering lights up a whole hospital ward: I recall a Christian with the wasting disease of disseminated sclerosis who had a phenomenal influence on the whole ward and nursing staff. Supremely, of course, the cross of Jesus Christ shows how much good can come out of suffering and apparent disaster. His death has proved the inspiration for millions of innocent sufferers as well as taking responsibility for the guilt of all who will turn to him.

But what troubled the group most were the natural disasters like earthquakes and famines. That is certainly the most difficult area of suffering for a Christian to explain. For we believe both that God is good and that God is loving: how then can such things be allowed in God's world? With other faiths the problem is not nearly so acute.

Christianity is not like Buddhism in seeing suffering as, in the final analysis, an illusion. The Bible sees it as agonizingly real.

Christianity is not like Hinduism in seeing suffering as an inevitable principle of retribution, the outworking of *karma*: you sin, you pay for it through suffering.

Christianity is not like Islam, relapsing into fatalism in the face of suffering: 'it is the will of Allah.' No, the Bible teaches that God does not willingly afflict us.

Christianity is not like modern Judaism in seeing suffering as atonement for sins. Christians realize that no man-made atonement can put us guilty human beings right with a holy God.

Nor is Christianity like atheism, in thinking of suffering as an inexplicable fact in a godless universe which we simply have to put up with.

For Christians the whole problem is more difficult. We believe in a Creator God who is both powerful and loving. Whence then, famines and earthquakes?

I think we have to begin with the link that the Bible makes between the fault line that runs through nature and the fault line that runs through human beings: they are linked, not only in the creation story but in our experience. We are belatedly coming to realize that this world is so precisely ordered that even small disturbance in one part of it can affect areas that are thousands of miles away: think of the so-called butterfly effect by which a large hatch of butterflies in Latin America can produce flooding in the Indian Ocean. Or think of the way that the destruction of the rainforests is having the most devastating effect on the world's climate. Think of the way emissions from our cars and fridges are piercing great holes in the protective ozone layer. Or think of Libya and Tunisia, once the great wheatfields of the Roman

Empire, but now irretrievable desert. The link between the damage to our environment and human mismanagement and greed is very evident.

Earthquakes generally take place along well-known fault lines in the earth's surface, where underlying plates overlap beneath the surface of the ground. I have recently seen a map showing where the earthquake hot spots were in the days of the dinosaurs; and superimposed upon it was a map of where they occur now. The plans are almost identical. Human beings have long known the dangers of living and building along such fault lines, but have continued to do it. Vancouver, where I worked for some years, is on the San Antonio fault line, and is sure to get a massive earthquake one day. If so, it would destroy the international airport, built only a few feet above sea level on a little island. But does that thought stop people building here? Not at all. And yet they will be sure to blame God when it comes! What's more, most of the devastation in earthquakes happens when poor materials or shoddy craftsmanship went into the erection of the houses – and that is a human failing. The buildings built to earthquake-proof specifications almost always withstand the quake.

Well, you may say, couldn't God have done a better job in creating the world? Two answers immediately come to mind. First, that the many supposed improvements on world design people have dreamed up since the days of the first-century BC Roman writer Lucretius have all been shown to be utterly unworkable. Any change would make things worse not better, so carefully balanced is our universe. And second, if we want a Christian explanation of suffering, we must go to the Bible.

The Bible makes it plain that the world as we know it is not as God originally made it, for human wickedness has affected the fabric of the created order. Nor is the world as it will one day be. It is a world in the making. God is ceaselessly working for the renewal and transformation of the world and has plans for its complete renewal. Pie in the sky? Not at all! That is demonstrated by the bodily resurrection of Jesus, where the stuff of his physical make-up, cruelly put to death, was raised with its constituent elements transformed so that it had new and more wonderful properties. It may help to see it as the change from petrol to energy: the same elements but different form. One day the 'new heaven and the new earth' which God plans will be like that. At present we must not complain if the created order does not manifest that same utter perfection as God its Creator. And earthquakes may be part of the seeming disorder in the world that actually are part of extremely complex solutions, to which we may at present be blind. After all, non-equilibrium is the source of balance!

But we must not miss the heart of the Christian teaching about God and suffering by concentrating too much on interesting but marginal parts of the problem of suffering like earthquakes. The utterly unique thing which Christianity reveals to the world is a suffering God. A God who understands our pain and frustration because he has willingly entered into it himself, and drained its anguish in the most excruciating death it is possible to devise, crucifixion. God may not have given us a perfect intellectual understanding of the mystery of suffering, but he has given us an awesome insight through the cross of Jesus into the sort of God he is. He is no blind despot pulling the wings off flies. He is not so far removed from the world that he does not care for our agonies. He is the God who came down onto the factory floor of the world and got his hands dirty. He suffered as we suffer, only more. On that cross the centre of his suffering was not the physical agony, but the anguish of carrying the load of the world's guilt: guilt which had not only separated us from God, but had affected the very fabric of the world we live in. And by that marvellous double act of Good Friday and Easter, he showed that sin and suffering would not have the last word in God's world. Tragedy will give way to triumph. It did for Jesus and it will for his people. Not necessarily in this life but after this life. For you can never get a proper handle on the problem of suffering if you restrict yourself to this life alone. This life, as Keats put it, is 'a vale of soul making', and it is in the life to come that we will be able to look back and say 'It was worth it.' And Jesus will be able to say 'Yes, I know. I have been through it too.' By far the wisest thing, then, for puzzled and suffering human beings to do is to bring their pain to the wounded hands and broken heart of the God-man who loved us and gave himself for us.

8. 'THERE ARE TOO MANY RELIGIONS IN THE WORLD FOR THEM ALL TO BE TRUE'

Karen works in a petrol station in south London. She was born and educated in a thoroughly multicultural community. She has several Asian friends, and a Hindu and a Muslim colleague.

She doesn't know much about their belief systems but has been aware of their different cultures for as long as she can remember. She admits to sometimes feeling resentful about what she views as her culture – English, white, Christian – being superseded by others that are less familiar, but she vigorously denounces racism.

Her grasp of interfaith issues is very slight, but her life-long awareness of multiculturalism has convinced her that since not all religious claims can be true, none of them is.

She is uncertain of this conclusion and almost debates it with herself in conversation. 'If there's only one God, why the hundreds of religions?' is her opening gambit. 'As you begin to appreciate all of the faiths, you understand that they've each got their own God . . . that's very hard to reconcile'.

When gently pressed on these ideas, however, she changes tack: 'Even though there are hundreds of religions, sometimes they do believe in the same thing. For example that there is someone higher up looking after them. The differences are because they've got different influences from different parts of the world.'

Part of her is inclined towards believing that all religions are essentially the same, though shaped by the various cultural influences inherent in their origins and development. She admits to not knowing enough about the particular beliefs to really help her answer these questions.

On final consideration, however, she changes tack again and refers to what she does feel confident she knows about religions to reach a (tentative) conclusion. 'Some of them believe that there are several gods and some that there is only one . . . some religions say that their god made the earth and then Christianity says their God made the earth. And, you know, someone's got to be lying.'

Response

Karen, I love the way you make your points about the great variety of faiths and cultures. You display an engaging modesty in your approach to this complicated issue. You are not embarrassed to backtrack and to change your mind at times, though your main point is very clear: they can't all be right!

Let's come to that main point in a minute. First, let us notice one or two very positive things. You yourself work among colleagues of different faiths, and they get along pretty well together. The same thing often (but not always) happens on the broader stage of world affairs. We live on rather a small planet, and unless we learn to get along with one another, there is precious little hope of survival, with all the sophisticated weapons of mass destruction we have invented.

Once I attended a remarkable meeting in HM Treasury. It was a day working on a plan to bring new hope to the poorest of the world's poor. There you found the President of the World Bank, the Chancellor of the Exchequer, the economist Lord Griffiths and the heads of big business, relief organizations like Oxfam and Tearfund, along with musicians like Bono and Bob Geldof. They were all united in determining to work to improve the state of the world's poor, by raising an additional $50 billion a year. Yes, but who else? You found the retired Archbishop of Canterbury, the Chief Rabbi, Cardinal Murphy O'Connor, the head of the Muslim council of Great Britain, the President of the National Council of Hindu Temples, the head of the Sikh Council for interfaith relations and many others. These leaders of the world's great faiths were united in a determination to do the right thing together, to eradicate extreme poverty, to create justice in trading, to remit crippling debt that can never be repaid, and so forth. So you see, Karen, the many faiths can unite for a noble purpose, and that is surely a good thing.

Having said that, as you point out, they can't all be right in what they believe. So a bit of clear thinking is in order.

First, it will not do to suppose it does not matter what you believe so long as you are sincere. I may sincerely believe that all roads from Oxford lead to London, or that a little cyanide on my porridge is good for me – but I should be wrong!

Second, it will not do to suppose that the religions are all basically saying the same thing. Karen, you were attracted by the idea that they all believe in someone up there looking after them. I'm afraid they don't. Buddhism, for example, does not believe in God at all. The Allah of Islam is very far away and you can never know him. In Satanism the ultimate force is evil not benevolent. In Hinduism there are many gods but behind them all there is one impersonal unity which certainly does not look after us. The sheer varieties of belief are completely irreconcilable.

Third, it will not do to suppose that all the religions are different roads going up the same hill and all will meet at the top. Buddhism believes you can save yourself by your noble deeds. Christianity believes your good deeds are never strong enough for that job: God alone has done all that is necessary to put us right with him. Hinduism believes that the principle of *karma* operates everywhere. It means 'you sin, you pay'. If you live a bad life now, you may come back in another life as a beetle. And only when you have worked your passage through many lives will you reach extinction. The Christian faith believes we have only one life, and our destiny is not extinction but to know God and enjoy him for ever. Unlike all the other faiths, it maintains that we are never going to be good enough for this great God, but that God in his great love has come to rescue us because he could not bear to have us separated from him for ever by the many evil choices we have consciously made.

Fourth, it will not do to pin our hopes on the baseless idea of all the roads leading up to the top of the same mountain. What if it is a false analogy? What if a better picture might be a maze, with lots of false turns in it and only one way to get out?

So how do we get any clear direction about the many religions?

Here's a suggestion. Why not start with looking into whether Jesus Christ is reliable? After all, we date our whole calendar from him. He has had more influence than any other great teacher. There really is no better way of finding out than to look into the story of this amazing person for yourself. I think you will probably find four things that set Jesus apart from any of the great religious leaders of the world and make him incomparably the greatest.

First, no great religious teacher other than Jesus even claimed to bring God before our gaze, let alone validated it by his life. C. S. Lewis expresses the difference well:

> There is no half-way house, and there is no parallel in other religions. If you had gone to Buddha and asked 'Are you the son of Bramah?' he would have said 'My son, you are still in the vale of illusion.' If you had gone to Socrates and asked

'Are you Zeus?' he would have laughed at you. If you had gone to Muhammad and asked 'Are you Allah?' he would first have rent his clothes and then cut off your head.

In sharp contrast to these other great teachers, Jesus claimed that he and his heavenly Father were one and the same, that if you wanted to see the Father you needed to take a long look at Jesus himself.[1] He claimed that 'no-one knows the Father except the Son and anyone to whom the Son chooses to reveal him' (Matthew 11:27). And then he went on to invite his hearers to come, not to the temple or to the law, but to himself: 'Come to me, all you that are weary and are carrying heavy burdens, and I will give you rest' (Matthew 11:28). Elsewhere he makes the most astonishing claims, that he is the Way to God, the Truth of God, the very Life of God:[2] that he is the bread without which we starve, and the wine without which we are parched.[3] We find him doing what the ancient scriptures had said only God could do, like stilling a mighty storm with a word,[4] raising a dead person to new life,[5] feeding a hungry multitude of five thousand with a few small loaves,[6] or offering divine forgiveness – and healing into the bargain – to a man who had lain paralysed for years.[7] Jesus backed his unique claims with unique deeds.

Second, nobody else among the great teachers has dealt satisfactorily with the problem of wickedness. Both Buddhism and Hinduism teach the inexorable law of *karma*: you have to bear the consequences for your misdeeds in another life. Islam predicts the fires of hell for all non-Muslims (Qur'an 74.27–29; 50.24–26; 78.21–30). Even Muslims can never be sure of acceptance with God, for 'Allah punishes whom he pleases and grants mercy to whom he pleases' (Qur'an 2.284). But Jesus' teaching on the subject was revolutionary. He said that he would give his life as a ransom to buy back the many who had been taken captive by evil.[8] And on the cross that is just what he did. He took personal responsibility for all the evil the world had done.[9] It broke his heart: it killed him. Because he was human like us, it was human beings paying the price, if you like. Because he was more than human, sharing God's nature, that offering of his is effective for all time.[10] Those who lived before Jesus and cast themselves on God's mercy, and those since his day who have done the same, all are accepted because not only is God love, but he is perfect justice as well.[11] The debt has been paid, the guilt has been purged or purified by that wonderful death of his on the cross to secure our pardon.

As if that was not enough, Jesus shows himself as the one you can really trust your life to because he is alive. The whole New Testament is alight with the confidence that Jesus is alive.[12] He is the Easter Jesus. He came back from the cold. He broke the power of the last and greatest enemy, death. He is alive, never to die again. What confidence that very well-attested resurrection can give us. Assurance that he really is the Son of God. Assurance that he really is the way to God. Assurance that his teaching is Truth. Assurance that he can give us new Life, both now and when we die. Nobody else among the religions of the world offers anything remotely comparable. No other great teacher came back from death as its conqueror. The bones of the Buddha are revered and divided up into 547 pieces throughout monasteries in South East Asia. The bones of Muhammad lie in Medina. But the bones of Jesus are nowhere to be found. As the first Christians put it, 'We know that Christ, being raised from the dead, will never die again; death no longer has dominion over him' (Romans 6:9). That fact alone would be sufficient to set him apart from all the other great teachers of the world.

And best of all, this Jesus offers to come and share the life of the believer. He is willing to come and be our constant companion, guide and friend. He has promised 'I will never leave you or forsake you' (Hebrews 13:5; cf. Matthew 28:20).

So, you see, it is not mere Christian prejudice that leads me to point you to Jesus. He offers these four great things which you can never find in any of the other religions of the world. So there is a lot of sense in recognizing that Christianity is not really a religion at all. Religion is something man-made, which is why there are so many of them. All of them offer their own way of attempting to get through to God. But the Christian gospel says that there is simply no way by which we can find God. He is too holy, pure and upright – and we are not. He is so great and we are so small. There is no way through. But in his love he has made a way through, a way back, and a way in! Real Christianity is not a religion but a revelation – showing us what God is like, through the person, the life and death of Jesus. It is also a rescue from the guilt and condemnation of the stuff in our past of which we are ashamed. Moreover, it is a relationship with him for ever.

That does not mean, Karen, that all other faiths have nothing helpful in them. They all have major strengths in their teachings, or they would never have attracted any worshippers. But if you want to get it sorted for yourself, why not explore the One who came to earth for the very purpose of getting to know and love and help you? There's only one person like that!

9. 'THERE'S NOT ENOUGH PROOF FOR ME TO BELIEVE'

Bernie is in his mid 20s and works in marketing. He has a degree in business studies and lives with friends in south London.

His work is essentially about decision-making: which campaigns should run using which media channels (television, radio, Internet, billboard, direct mail, etc.), for how long and costing how much. It can be something of a minefield, he admits, with the best chance of success coming from gathering and analysing the most accurate information – about consumer attitudes, media consumption, budgetary limitations – available.

He has little interest in matters religious or spiritual, with work, football and socializing taking up the lion's share of his life. He is earning good money, living with friends and in good health and has no 'hole in his life' to be filled.

He has little to say about religion, knowing very little about traditional religions. He describes himself as agnostic, not knowing enough to make him believe or disbelieve. The truth is, he admits, he doesn't really care enough.

He can, however, talk about the idea of believing which, in his work, is the word people use when they don't really know the answer. Belief, as far as he is concerned, is just not good enough.

'I don't say that I don't believe in it. I don't say that I do believe it,' he says. 'I think until a proof has been shown to me . . . there's too many missing links.' He is not entirely clear on what 'it' is but he is sure that it is unproven, and therefore unreliable. 'A lot of it, I think, well all of it is unproven, so you don't know whether to believe in it or not.'

When pressed on what proof he might want, it becomes clear that for him, proof is actually synonymous with tangible evidence.

*'There's no concrete and no physical evidence is there?' he says.
'It's hard to believe anything where you can't actually prove it to
yourself.'*

*He seems to think that religious claims demand complete and
unquestioning acquiescence and, in one unsure moment, refers to
'doubting Thomas' to explain this.*

*'In the Bible you've got the doubting Thomas thing, haven't
you? That's their [i.e. religious people's] card, isn't it? [To] those
people who don't believe, people [who] want evidence. Doubting
Thomas . . . there's a little story to stop people wanting evidence all
the time. It's wrong to want it. You've just got to believe it, you've
got to have faith.'*

*As far as Bernie is concerned, religious faith is untenable
because it is not based on any evidence, certainly nothing like the
research and statistics he deals with at work. Belief is unjustifiable
because it is not proof.*

Response

Bernie, let's get a few things straight. First of all about proof.
Nothing worthwhile in life is provable in the sense you are
after. Indeed you cannot prove that your mother loves you
or even that you are alive. There is good evidence for these
things, of course, and you act on the evidence all the time.
Well, I have written about the nature of proof and the solid
evidence that points to the existence of God in chapter 12,
at the end of this book. Nick Spencer's survey deliberately
excluded those who were sure God existed and also those
who were sure he did not. He concentrated on the great
majority of the British population who currently do not go
anywhere to worship and are negative or very unsure about
the claims of the Christian faith. But I should be failing in my
task if I did not go beyond his self-imposed limits, and say

something to those who were very dubious about the existence of God. I offer these seven facts, not theories or beliefs,
but seven facts which individually point in the direction
of God's reality, and when taken together make an overwhelming case. I suggest you read that chapter, Bernie. I
think you will get much clearer about the nature and limitations of proof than you at present appear to be. And I do not
think you will be able to maintain that there is no evidence,
upon which you can base a rational decision.

So in this chapter, I am going to turn to the evidence for
Jesus being the Son of God. You admit that you do not know
(or care) much about it. But if you decide that he really is
God's special messenger or representative who has come
to show us what God is like and has gone to the anguish of
crucifixion to bring us back to God – well, you may want
to change your attitude. In any case I want to confront you
with the evidence, because evidence is what you are looking
for.

Let's get it clear to begin with, that Jesus is a historical
figure. There is far more evidence for his existence than
there is for Julius Caesar, for example. It is not only the
Gospels and letters of the New Testament, and an unbroken
chain of writers since then. We have both Jewish and Roman
writers of the time who tell us about Jesus.

The Roman historian Tacitus, who wrote at the end of
the first century, talks about the Fire of Rome in AD 64 and
rejects the smear that the Christians had started it. He says,
'The name of Christians comes to them from Christ who
was executed in the reign of Tiberius by the Procurator
Pontius Pilate' (*Annals* 15.44). Pliny, writing a decade later,
speaks of the enormous advance of the Christian cause in
north Turkey where he was governor. He tells us that the
only bizarre thing he could find about the Christians was that

they met early in the morning and 'sang a hymn to Christ as God' and they refused to bow down to the Emperor's statue and deny the name of Jesus (Pliny, *Letters* 10.96).

The Jewish author Josephus, writing at the end of the first century, has an astonishing piece about Jesus which is worth quoting since it is so remarkable for a Jew to write it.

> There arose about that time [i.e. Pilate's time, AD 26–36] Jesus, a wise man, if indeed we should call him a man, for he was a doer of marvellous deeds, a teacher of men who receive the truth with pleasure. He won over many Jews and also many Greeks. This man was the Messiah. And when Pilate had condemned him to the cross at the instigation of our own leaders, those who loved him from the first did not cease. For he appeared to them on the third day alive again, as the holy prophets had predicted and said many other wonderful things about him. And even now the race of Christians, so named after him, has not died out. (*Antiquities* 18.3)

Some people find these words so astounding coming from a Jew that they suspect he can't have written them. But they are in all copies of the text of Josephus!

So let's not pretend there is no secular evidence about Jesus! Actually, if you amass it all together it gives us a remarkable confirmation of what we read in the Gospels. The secular and Jewish sources tell us that Jesus had a most remarkable birth. He had a brother called James. He worked miracles. He had disciples who were called Christians, and who worshipped him as God. He said he would die and then return again. He was executed by Pilate, on a day when the sky turned black at Passover time. He rose from the tomb and was seen by his followers. Christianity rapidly spread to Rome, Alexandria and Asia Minor and became a worldwide movement. His essential message was embodied in the letters of the Greek word for a fish meaning 'Jesus Christ, Son of God, Saviour', which was found all over the Roman Empire.

But of course the best evidence is the Gospels, which have come down to us from first-century companions of Jesus and their colleagues. You might care to check out chapter 5 above, which looks into them a bit more carefully. The fact is that there is overwhelming evidence to show to any open-minded person that Jesus was a real person, who brought God into our midst in terms we could really understand (the terms of a human life), that his death on the cross did all that was necessary to bring guilty folk like you and me back to God, and that he is alive again, gloriously alive. It would have been impossible otherwise for the church to get started. There were lots of so-called messiahs in the politically frenetic atmosphere of first-century Judea: the Romans executed them efficiently, their followers disappeared, and the whole thing was forgotten until the next one turned up. Not so with Jesus. This executed Galilean peasant teacher rose from the dead, and two thousand years later more than a third of the world worships him as God.

The fact is, Bernie, that there is nothing wrong with the evidence. Are you sure it's not the case that you don't want to face it?! It might make a difference to your life, and you are quite happy as you are, thanks very much. You may be one of the 37% of British people who (at the time of writing!) think a footballer like David Beckham is more important than God. But in the long run that is a very short-sighted policy. Because one of these days we are all going to die. Then the God who gave us life will call us to account for how we have used it. We are going to face the judgment of God on our lives. The Bible says 'it is appointed for mortals to die once and after that the judgment'. It says 'all of us must appear before the judgment seat of Christ' (Hebrews 9:27; 2 Corinthians 5:10). What if that is true, Bernie? It's not worth taking a chance on it. Are you going to say to God 'Sorry I didn't bother about you. I did not think there was enough evidence!'? Would not God be justified in replying,

> I gave you the evidence of a beautiful world that I had made. I gave you the evidence of a moral conscience, pointing to me. I gave you the supreme evidence of my Jesus who came for you. He died for you, he is alive for you, and he has been asking for admission to your life for decades. And you tell me there is no evidence? You do not even bother to look into it, because you are so caught up in your football, your friends and your comfortable lifestyle. You work at advertising products that will soon be out of date, and checking consumer attitudes that will soon be irrelevant. Whose fault will it be if you simply do not bother to check out the evidence for the truth of the Christian story?

If you decide that this story is true, then it is clearly the most important thing in the world: there is a God and he cares for you and looks for your response. But if you find it is not true, then feel free to rubbish it relentlessly. Attack Christianity for all you are worth! But don't remain satisfied to describe yourself as an agnostic who simply does not care enough to find out. After all, your job, you say, is about decision making!

And just one thing more, Bernie. In your profession you naturally see faith or belief as an inferior form of knowledge. That is not what Christian faith is. It is not a poor substitute for knowledge at all. Faith means trust, like in a good marriage. As a matter of fact everyone has faith in something:

maybe in a partner, or perhaps in a theory like the theory of evolution, or even faith in the chair they are sitting on. Each of these has an element of self-commitment about it, but only when the evidence warrants it. You mention the Thomas story in the Gospels. I reckon you've got Thomas all wrong! It isn't, as you put it, 'a little story to stop people wanting evidence . . . You've just got to believe it, you've got to have faith.' That is not what the Thomas story is saying. It's well worth looking into carefully.[1] Thomas didn't believe Jesus had been raised from the dead. He didn't believe his mates who assured him that they had met the risen Jesus. He wanted the tangible evidence that you too are after. He got it. Jesus stood before him, with the marks of the nail-wounds in his hands and the spear-wound in his side, and said, 'Peace be with you'. He wants to say the same to you and me. He invited Thomas to put his finger in the holes in his hands, and his hand into the hole in his side, and to throw away his doubts and believe (i.e. trust, commit himself). I don't for a moment suppose Thomas did that. He was down on his face on the floor, no doubt weeping his eyes out and saying 'My Lord and my God!'.

It is interesting that the author makes this incident the climax of his Gospel. He tells us why a few verses later. He recorded this very tangible proof among many other evidential signs in his Gospel for two reasons. He wanted his readers to 'come to believe that Jesus is the Messiah, the Son of God'. And he wanted them – and you – to go on from there and commit themselves to Jesus, so that 'believing you may have life in his name' (John 20:31). Bernie, get that Gospel of John on your reading list!

10. 'SOMETHING 2,000 YEARS OLD CAN'T BE RELEVANT TO ME TODAY'

Chloe is very conscious of her generation. She has grown up in a 'technotopia', never having known a world without personal computers, mobiles, the Internet, digital television, DVDs and games consoles. Existence before these gadgets is almost inconceivable to her.

She has recently turned 20 and lives with her parents in a wealthy suburb of Nottingham while she studies. She is excited by life, has a wide circle of friends, enough money to socialize, and the prospect of a good job when she qualifies. Religious faith does not even feature on her radar.

Unsurprisingly, it takes quite an effort for her to talk about Christianity, not because she isn't intelligent, but because she has never really thought about religion and has no real opinion about it.

Her knowledge of Christianity (and indeed of all religions) is close to non-existent. She knows it is about God and about Jesus but that is about it.

She has more to say when questioned about why she thinks so few people attend church these days.

'Religion is different for our generation than it was for older generations,' she says. 'They were perhaps brought up not to question things so much, so they would go to church because their parents told them to . . . we have been brought up to question society or question whatever and make up our own minds, and so we are not so inclined to go to church without knowing'.

She has a great deal of respect for her parents, but in her heart she believes that the world has moved too fast for them and their generation. Theirs was a world, she thinks, of credulousness and obedience, whereas hers is one of scepticism and rebellion. Without saying it in as many words, she feels their attitudes to life are pretty much out-of-date today.

This train of thought leads her back to the religious claims themselves. If her parents' generation is already outdated, how much more are the beliefs of people who lived hundreds or thousands (she's not quite sure of the right date) of years ago?

'I would agree that a lot of the rules that were set out so many thousands or millions of years ago or whatever, they are not really as relevant in today's society,' she says. That was then, she believes. This is now. And while she is open-minded and non-judgmental about whether such rules were a good thing at the time, it is inconceivable to her that they could possibly be relevant today.

'The story behind it all just doesn't interest me at all. It's just what I believe about here and now, you know.'

Response

'That was then. This is now.' That is a splendid and fairly typical attitude in a 20-year old who has money, friends and good prospects. God and church have never got under her radar. The parents are well-meaning oldies. They didn't have the critical acumen or the adult toys that we have nowadays. Interestingly enough, this attitude is new: no previous generation has made so radical a disjunction between their age and what has gone before.

I confess I have a soft spot for the vitality, the self-confidence and the gentle dismissiveness of such a world-view. But it really won't do, and I fancy, Chloe, that as you grow older you will find it simply isn't true. Major events in the past are relevant because they helped to shape our present world. For example, you would not be able to go to the hospital for free were it not for the founding of the National Health Service. In any case, human nature is pretty much a constant throughout recorded history. Two thousand years ago the shape of society may have been very different, but human needs and concerns, hopes and fears, purpose and identity remain the same today. And real Christianity speaks to those concerns today just as much as it did two thousand years ago.

There's another thing. The scepticism which you charmingly regard as the discovery of your generation was there among the ancient Greeks six hundred years before Christ, and has been a major mark of European thought since Descartes in the seventeenth century. It lies at the heart of scientific method. It simply means we are determined to evaluate evidence critically, and not be taken for a ride by believing myths. And that makes admirable sense.

I think, too, that you are making a further mistake in imagining that something two thousand years ago could not be of relevance to you. The present is shaped by the past. The Big Bang is estimated to have taken place between five and fifteen billion years ago, and yet it has such impact on your life that had it not happened, neither would you! But you have a point. An event long ago in the past, if it was *just* an event in the past, is indeed irrelevant to a lively young woman like you. But an event that, like the Big Bang, has continued impact on all subsequent life is far from irrelevant. Christians claim that the coming, dying, and rising of the Son of God is comparable to the Big Bang. It is God's act of re-creation, and like the Big Bang has a lasting impact on all who come after.

You may not see it this way because, on your own showing, you have so far had no experience of Christianity. You just 'know it is about God and Jesus and that is about it'. You are right, of course, but there is rather more to it than that. How could we ever know about God, whether he exists and what he is like? There is no sure way, unless he came to show us. Christians down the centuries have believed, on good evidence which we have looked at in chapter 9, that God has done just that. Jesus is not merely a wonderful man, but the human embodiment of God: as much of God, if you like, as could be crammed into human form. His matchless life, his unparalleled teaching, his staggering claims, his fulfilment of scores of ancient prophecies, his love for one and all, his purity, his self-sacrifice all substantiate that claim. But there is one clinching argument. The apostle Paul, himself a reluctant convert from blood-thirsty opposition to Jesus Christ, alludes to it in his letter to Roman Christians.[1] Jesus, he claims, was defined as Son of God powerfully by his resurrection from the dead. That resurrection, if it is true, sets him apart from all other great religious teachers throughout history. He predicted, so the Gospels tell us, that he would be cruelly mistreated, crucified and rise again from the dead.[2] And it happened. The whole Christian faith is built on that resurrection of Jesus Christ from the grip of death on the first Easter Day.

So, Chloe, instead of complaining that nothing two thousand years ago could be faintly relevant to you today, take a long look at the resurrection of Jesus Christ. If it is true, he is alive for ever more. Alive for you personally. He can be your companion through life, your guide, your friend and can welcome you when you are no longer 20, and even when the cold waters of death close over you. If it is true, it is profoundly relevant. But is it? That is where you need to get your critical streak to work!

Your position is very much like mine when, as a successful and confident teenager, I heard an old man solemnly telling a group of my peers, gathered in a sports pavilion, that Jesus Christ was alive. I thought it was ridiculous, and I asked who the speaker was. I found out he was the Professor of Surgery at Bristol University and the editor of the *British Medical Journal*! I realized that he could not be off his head: if he was persuaded that Jesus was alive, I must at least look into it. I did. And I could not help being persuaded. In due course I entrusted myself to him, and since then companionship with that risen Jesus has profoundly changed my life.

It has been like that with countless people I have known. One good example is a car thief who came to Christ when lying in a pool of blood after being beaten up by the warders in gaol. He cried out 'Gawd 'elp me!' and Gawd did! Shortly afterwards the prison chaplain came in and showed him the way to Jesus. In due course, a couple of years after his release, he was accepted by the Church of England for training as a clergyman, and he came to the college where I was the principal. He had a very colourful and effective way of explaining the gospel, and was ordained to work in a rough mining district in Nottinghamshire. His whole life was transformed. As a crook, his great aim had been to get something for nothing. His new goal as a Christian minister was to earn a wage in order to sustain his family, offer hospitality to others, and introduce them to the Jesus who had changed his own life. That's the sort of difference Jesus Christ makes when you put yourself into his hands.

So yes, the proof of the pudding is in the eating. Jesus can be very relevant today. But can we really believe he rose from the dead? Is it possible that he is alive and able to help us today? Let's take a look at the evidence.

Contemporary accounts in the four Gospels, the letters of the apostles Paul, Peter and John make it abundantly clear that Jesus was crucified in a very public execution on the cross. He was placed in a rock-hewn tomb, the tomb was sealed up, and a guard of soldiers was placed over it. This seems to have been because various hints of resurrection Jesus had given throughout his ministry might have encouraged grave robbers to steal the body and claim he was risen. As a matter of fact, a few people have made claims like this, notably Hugh Schonfield in his book *The Passover Plot*. But the idea that a crucified man could revive in the cool of the tomb and be spirited away, despite a rock on the entrance and a guard outside, is preposterous. We actually know for sure he was dead. Not only because Romans were expert at the grisly task of crucifixions and nobody ever survived, but because one of the Gospel writers mentioned something which amazed him but which he could not understand: when a spear was thrust under the heart of Jesus to make sure he was dead, out came 'blood and water' (John 19:33–35). The science of the day was not advanced enough to realize that the separation of dark red clot from light coloured serum is the strongest proof of death! So the resurrection is strongly supported by the fact that the tomb was found empty on the first Easter Day, the third after his execution. What's more, the winding sheet packed with spices that had been put round his body was still in place, along with the turban wound round his head.[3] Jesus had gone. He had been raised into a new form of existence. Who would have left the grave clothes all wound around like an empty chrysalis case if they had stolen the body?!

But the evidence for the resurrection does not depend on an empty tomb, but on a living Jesus, a Jesus whom people met after his resurrection. And there were hundreds of them, people who knew him well. The fishermen, the women who had accompanied his mission, his close associates. Our earliest account of the resurrection mentions 'more than five hundred brothers and sisters' who saw him on a single occasion. Most of them, we read, were still alive when the record was penned in the early fifties AD, though some had died.[4] None of them was easily taken in: there is a note of initial incredulity in all the accounts, as you will see if you read the resurrection story in the four Gospels. But they were persuaded, and once persuaded they could not keep quiet. Nothing like this had ever been known since the foundation of the world. They had found the key to life! Interestingly, one of Jesus' disciples, Thomas, was absent the first time Jesus appeared to the others. He flatly disbelieved the story. But as we saw in chapter 9, Jesus appeared again, face to face with Thomas, and he fell down at the feet of Jesus with the strongest confession of faith to be found anywhere in the New Testament, 'My Lord and my God!' Or think of Saul of Tarsus, the scourge of Christians, who chased them from city to city and slaughtered them. That man, renamed Paul, became the strongest Christian evangelist there has ever been. And it happened because he met with the risen Christ, and gratefully surrendered to him.

What fascinates me is the difference he made to such people. As we have just seen, the risen Jesus turned Saul of Tarsus from a bitter opponent to a joyful and passionate follower, who in due course gave his life for the cause of Christ. James, a brother in Jesus' family, did not believe in Jesus while he was alive. But after his death and resurrection we find James leading the early church in Jerusalem. How come? Paul has a succinct answer to that: 'he appeared to James' (1 Corinthians 15:7). Simon Peter, the bombastic fisherman who was always talking big but achieving little during the days when Jesus was around, now, after the resurrection becomes a man of rock, taking on the whole Jewish religious establishment. He fearlessly preached that 'this

Jesus God raised up, and of that all of us are witnesses' (Acts 2:32). These renewed followers of Jesus went and founded churches all over the Roman world. They were over the moon with their discovery that guilt and death did not hold all the aces. On the contrary, their Jesus had trumped the lot. He had dealt with evil by taking its consequences on himself. He was alive for evermore, the conqueror of death and companion of those who would trust him. And the more you persecuted these Christians and killed them, the more the movement spread. Precisely the same thing is happening today in places like Tanzania, China, Nigeria – to name but three. The risen Jesus Christ can be known and enjoyed by anyone. And the Christian gospel is spreading worldwide today faster than it ever has before. People who have met Jesus cannot keep quiet about him.

You see, Chloe, it's not all about some event in the past that is irrelevant to you and me. The dynamic impact of that historic event remains. The tomb was empty. Jesus rose from the dead and he met lots of people. He changed their lives, giving them a tremendous new joy, moral power and courage, together with a glorious hope for death and beyond. Listen to Simon Peter on the subject. 'Blessed be the God and Father of our Lord Jesus Christ! By his great mercy he has given us a new birth into a living hope through the resurrection of Jesus Christ from the dead' (1 Peter 1:3). And it was not just that first generation. He has been doing it ever since. He has done it for me. I have seen him make contact with people on every continent and start changing their lives for the better. There is no reason why he should not do it for you, if only you will ask him to come and start living in you. You say you are excited by life. Good. But until you get linked up with the life of Jesus, 'you ain't seen nothing yet'!

11. 'IF THERE IS A GOD, WHY DOESN'T HE JUST SEND SOMEONE DOWN?'

Of all of the different reasons for unbelief discussed in the various interviews, one in particular came up most often and was most intensely felt. Few of those interviewed expressed more than a handful of the sentiments discussed above, and for many of those there was a tension between what they wanted to believe and what they thought was credible. 'My head tells me there isn't a God but my heart wants to believe in it,' one explained. 'Without having that higher plane or greater being, you'd never have hope. Hope would be pointless. Why would you hope or wish for something?', remarked another.

In spite of this yearning, the reasons not to believe were, at least for this group of people, too strong, with the most difficult problem being that of suffering.

As already noted, people's attitude to suffering varied, some blaming God for everything, some blaming him for natural disasters, some blaming human beings for most things, some blaming religion in particular.

Underlying many of the complaints and intellectual problems was a personal, emotional issue. The problem was at least as much about the way my heart feels as the way my mind thinks. And in spite of recognizing the cause of at least some of the world's suffering, those who were interviewed had little to suggest about what should be done, short of demanding peace rather than war, and tolerance rather than intolerance.

In the midst of such discussions, God was criticized and 'called on' several times, with one of the most poignant moments being when someone, earnestly and almost desperately, said, 'There's so much war and conflict. If there is a God, why doesn't he just send someone down?'

Response

Of all the responses Nick's survey unearthed, this was the most moving. It was a cry from the heart. How right it was to observe that, without having a higher plane or a greater being we could have no lasting hope. Short-term hopes, yes. But in the end all our hopes would crumble to ashes with the approach of death. If there is no God, Shakespeare would be right in seeing life as 'a tale told by an idiot, full of sound and fury, indicating nothing'. Hope is one of the most fundamental characteristics of our lives. Without hope we cannot live fulfilled lives.

But what about this poignant hope that there might be a God who would send someone down? Is this just one more hope doomed to come to nothing? 'My head tells me to believe there is no God, but my heart wants to believe in it' was the cry. But does our head really tell us there is no God? Do we really have to throw our brains away if we become Christians? In the final chapter of this book I offer you a number of solid facts which point very clearly to the existence and nature of God. But here I'd like to take a different tack.

Just suppose for a moment that the vast majority of humankind across the world and down the ages is right, and there is a God, a supreme source of our world and of ourselves, from which all else flows. Take a flight of imagination and think what it would be like if you yourself were this God. After all, if the author and actress Shirley MacLaine could claim to be God, why not you? Now what would you do if you wanted to reach out in love to the human beings you had made in your own likeness, but who did not want to know you? How would you get through to men or women in revolt who swore black and blue that you did not exist?

You might begin by creating a marvellous *world*, which shouted out the love and skill, the power and beauty of the Creator. Well perhaps God has done just that.

Then you might create *people* who were capable of responding to love. People with the dangerous gift of free will, able either to respond to you or to reject you. Well, maybe God took the risk and did that too.

You could then go on to instil in the hearts of these people *values* which spoke of God. Values like truth, goodness, beauty, harmony, creativity, speech, love. Of course you could never force virtue on them. Free agents, they could choose the opposite – and people often do. But wherever they are found, these qualities would point to the Giver, the one who is absolute truth, perfect goodness, unutterable beauty, complete harmony, unceasing creativity, and the very source both of communication and of love. Such qualities would be the imprint of the God who leaves his footprints in the sand of our lives. Might God have done that?

You might like the idea of building in a *conscience*, which would alert your creatures to right and wrong. A conscience which would approve when they chose the right way, and would prod and warn them when they went astray from your will – which is no arbitrary whim but their highest good. A conscience which would persevere however much they tried to stifle it. Could God have done that too?

You could after that instil *a God-shaped blank* into their lives, a hole which nothing else could fill apart from God himself. A space which cried out for satisfaction and fulfilment however much rubbish they crowd into it. A space that would elicit from them the cry which came to Augustine's lips centuries ago, 'O God you have made us for yourself, and our hearts are restless until they find their rest in you.' God has done that too, has he not? You said so yourself: 'My heart wants to believe in it.'

You might then, if you were God, show your hand in the *course of history*. You might ensure that the arrogance of nations and civilizations led inevitably to corruption and fall. You might concentrate on one man to begin with, then one family, one tribe, one nation which would trust you and obey you, and which in time you could train to receive and perhaps even follow your directions for their highest good. They might have to go through war and captivity as they learned those lessons, but because the stakes were high, you would persevere with them and take great pains over them. So much would depend on their understanding and their lifestyle if you were going to be able to really get through to them, and then through them reach out to a whole lost world that was out of touch with you. Isn't that precisely what God did with the Jewish people in the centuries leading up to Christ?

Finally, just conceivably, you might decide to *come in person* to their world. You would have to come as one of them, of course, for if you disclosed yourself in all your radiant beauty they would be blinded by the sight. You would need to arrive softly, and in disguise. You would need to learn their language so perfectly, without the trace of a foreign accent, that you could easily be mistaken for a native. It would be immensely costly. You would have to love them an awful lot if you were going to shrink yourself down to their level. It would be rather like one of us voluntarily turning into a rat or a slug – in order really to communicate effectively with such lowly creatures. It would be an almost unthinkable sacrifice. But what if God did that too?

And just supposing your love for them was boundless, you might even take one further step, *rescue*. Remember, they are out of touch with you because of the wrong things they have thought and done, and the wrong attitude towards you they have taken up. That must matter to you, You can't pretend all is well. It is not. They are in the wrong with you. They are guilty. They are cut off. But have you taken all that trouble in getting in touch with them only to leave them in the lurch? Surely not. You will come to the rescue, cost what it may. Long ago you had instilled in your people that if humans determine to cut themselves off from you, you will ratify their choice. They will get what they want. You will respect the freedom of their choice even in the hell of their own choosing. Very well, if you were utterly determined to broker reconciliation, you might even determine to die that death on behalf of all people, to carry in your own person that guilt which everyone shares, to pay that ransom price to set us all free. The precise imagery is comparatively unimportant. The fact – if true – is the most important in all the world. There is a living God and he loves his people that much! Could God have done that too?

It was the conviction that God had done precisely that which fired the early Christians. A handful of peasants, originally, they in due course engulfed the Roman Empire and became the largest religion the world has ever seen, embracing a third of humankind . . . and still growing with many thousand new believers every day. The longings of the hearts of these Christians was matched by the confidence of their minds. The Great Lover, the Great Reconciler had come. He had died for them. He was alive for them. They knew him. And there was nothing so important as to revel in that relationship and pass it on to others.

We have looked at some of the evidence for who Jesus was and his resurrection from the dead in the past two chapters. Surely now is the time for you to do something about it. You will always be torn between heart and head until you surrender yourself to the God who gave you both. If you want the longings of your heart and the workings of your mind to come together in a harmonious balance, there is a step to be taken, a step that cannot be avoided. It is to come back to God and admit that you have kept him out. Admit that your attitude of independence from him has led to bad things in your behaviour, your habits and your relationships. There is no way that we can approach a holy God without a genuine 'Sorry' on our lips – and in our hearts.

I think you will find that that 'Sorry' leads to real joy, and gratitude too. You will have realized by now that this is no dream, but solid reality: so solid that you could have bruised your toes on the cradle in Bethlehem or got splinters in your hand from the cross at Calvary. And you will want to thank God with all your heart that he has bothered about you, come for you, died for you, and is alive for you. Indeed, at the end of your road, he has undertaken to welcome you home. You know it won't be easy to be a follower of Jesus, a real Christian, in a society that often ignores him, but you are prepared for that. Of course you will need to team up with other followers of Jesus. But first and foremost you need to tell him that you are gladly accepting that most gracious offer of his: 'Listen! I am standing at the door, knocking; if you hear my voice and open the door, I will come in' (Revelation 3:20). You have heard his voice in your heart – yes, and in your mind as well? You long to experience the reality of it all for yourself? Then invite the Lord to come and share your very being. Ask his unseen risen life, what the Bible calls his Holy Spirit, to come into your life, just as you would invite a friend to enter your home. 'Come in,' you would say, as you unlock the door. 'Great to see you. Sorry about the mess. Have a coffee.' Those words in Revelation 3:20 make it crystal clear that the Lord himself will come in, he will accept your hospitality, and he will never leave you. And as for the mess – why, he is the man with the vacuum cleaner!

12. 'THAT IS ALL VERY WELL, BUT I'M NOT SURE I BELIEVE IN GOD'

Let's remind ourselves where these varied objections to the Christian faith have taken us. The climate of our society is decidedly post-Christian, so it is very understandable that many people do not take the time and trouble to look into the claims of Christianity. They see no reason to do so, because the image they have got of the church is unattractive. After all, we want to make the most of life, and the church seems so inflexible and dull. We want to express ourselves, and the church doesn't cater for that: its services seem dominated by a predetermined pattern. We have expressed considerable sympathy with the observation that you don't need to go to church to be spiritual, and that some churchgoers seem to be hypocrites. But although there is something in these objections, they are not compelling.

We looked at the question of tolerance, almost the only virtue that is still admired today. And we have seen that if Christians seem intolerant it is usually because of their loyalty to the teaching of Jesus Christ – and that is surely understandable enough.

We then moved on to some very substantive issues. Can we trust the Bible? Has science disproved Christianity? What about the problems of suffering and the multiplicity of religions in the world? And is evidence for the life, death and resurrection of Jesus Christ solid enough to warrant our allegiance? We reflected on the limitations of proof. We examined the very modern idea that if something is old it cannot be relevant, and found that to be a mistake. And finally we responded to the marvellous question, 'If there is a God, why doesn't he just send someone down?' There is only one faith in the world that claims God has done just that. It is the Christian faith.

But I suspect that although we may appreciate the responses that have been given to such questions as these, which haunt many people's minds, there is that lurking suspicion that there may not be enough evidence for us to believe in God at all. So before I shut down my computer I want to say something to those of my readers who are tending towards atheism, because that seems to them to be the most likely explanation of ourselves and our world.

If you go by the television or the conversations in the pub, you might think that atheism constitutes a large sample in British society. As a matter of fact it is rather a small one, scoring a mere 10% in the 1998 survey done by the Office for National Statistics. Statistics cannot determine the truth or otherwise of belief in God, but at least they show that believers are not a tiny remnant compared with atheists.

Let's begin by reminding ourselves again of the limited usefulness of proof. You can neither prove God nor disprove him. You can't prove your partner loves you. In fact there are precious few things you can prove, and they are by no means the most interesting aspects of life. To prove a thing means to show that it could not be otherwise, and that is a very final form of certainty. You cannot prove the sun will rise tomorrow. You cannot actually prove that you are alive. You cannot prove you are the same person you were ten years ago. The philosopher David Hume attempted to prove the link between himself and the man he was ten years previously – and he utterly failed! Proof only applies to rarified areas of mathematics and philosophy. For the rest we have to work on good evidence. There is very good evidence for our existence, for our identity, and for supposing that the sun will rise tomorrow. And there is good reason to believe in God. Indeed, the evidence is so good that it is much harder to reject God's existence than to accept it.

Very well, let's have a look at the evidence. I am not going to offer you theories or impressions but facts. Let us see where they point.

1. The fact of the world

Reflect on the world. So far as we know at present, this planet is the only part of the universe where there is conscious life. What accounts for this world of ours? Most scientists have abandoned the 'Steady State' theory of the origin of the universe in favour of the 'Big Bang'. But we can't leave it there. We cannot help asking what lay behind the Big Bang. What caused it? If the answer is in terms of atoms, molecules and DNA, the question must be pressed: why should they possess the remarkable properties they do? Why should there be any atoms rather than none? And why should DNA be the individual and unique key to everybody on earth? We all know that nothing comes from nothing. Every finite thing is caused. To put it in philosophical terms, all contingent facts must, in the final analysis, be based on a necessary cause. If you deny that, you have real problems in suggesting how this highly sophisticated world originated. You may say 'Evolution'. That will scarcely do. Even if the theory of evolution were universally accepted among scientists, you would need to have an adequate starting point for the evolutionary process. Darwin himself, at the outset of *The Origin of Species*, acknowledged God as that source. Nor can we escape from the necessity of God by saying 'Well, it is sheer chance. Just one of those things.' If the world was due to chance, how come that cause and effect are built into it at every turn? It is not very rational to suppose that chance gives rise to cause and effect. And it is not very rational to suggest that the world which is based on cause and effect is itself uncaused. Huxley once said 'The link between cause and effect is the chief article of the scientist's creed.' 'If you think hard enough', said the Oxford biologist Professor Sir Alister Hardy, 'science itself drives you back to belief in a Creator.'

2. The fact of design

Reflect on the fact of design in the world. At every level, nature shows evidence of design. Think of the focusing equipment of the eye, the intricacy of the ear, the radar of a bat, the built-in gyroscope of a swallow or the camouflage of a pheasant. Or think of the perfect harmony of the laws of physics. Reflect on the marvel of conception and birth. At every point there is evidence of a great Designer. Modern science is recognizing this as the anthropic principle. It means that had the circumstances of our physical world been a fraction different, life could not have existed on this planet. It seems to be custom-made for human life! As Professor John Polkinghorne put it, 'There is a very tight-knit series of constraints . . . on the way our world must be in order that we are here to observe it'. Even John Stuart Mill, a strong opponent of Christianity, came to this con-clusion at the end of his life. 'The argument from design is irresistible,' he said. 'Nature does testify to its Creator.' Professor Paul Davies, the distinguished New Zealand physi-cist, writes: 'The well-defined laws of physics, and definite cause and effect relationships, reveal a level of order and symmetry in the universe that demand some sort of cosmic design.' Einstein, too, spoke of his 'humble admiration of the illimitably superior Spirit who reveals himself in the slight details which we can perceive with our frail minds'. Physicists operate on the assumption of consistency and design in the universe. Very well, if there is design, where did it come from? Not from us. We don't lay down the laws of nature or design the development of the foetus in the womb. It very much looks as if a Designer is at work. The argument from design is highly persuasive, and to say with Jean-Paul Sartre, 'This world is not the product of intelligence. It meets our gaze as would a crumpled piece of paper ... What is man but a little puddle of water whose freedom is death?' is to shut your eyes to one of the clearest indications that there is a Creator God who has not left himself without witness. 'The heavens are telling the glory of God; and the firmament proclaims his handiwork' remains true: so does the Bible's assertion, 'Fools say in their hearts, "There is no God"' (Psalms 19:1; 14:1).

3. The fact of personality

Look at the fact of personality. It is one of the most remarkable phenomena in the world. The difference between a person and a thing, between a live person and a dead one, is fundamental. When Sartre, in the quotation given above, denied that the world was created by Intelligence, he was not only insulting his Maker (as he admitted at the very end of his life) but his own powers of reasoning. He was saying in effect that there was no reason to believe what he was saying! The fact is that we are not mere robots: there is more to us than that – human personality. The medical student can, no doubt, analyse his girlfriend into calcium, water, fat and so forth. But he chooses her for other reasons – because she is a person he admires. You cannot reduce love and emotions, resolve and decision-making to chemistry. We are not mere matter. But the alternative is disturbing. It suggests that my personality cannot be explained simply in terms of its physical components alone. I am more than matter. But how could that be if there is no God? Does a river flow higher than its source? Of course not. Then how do we get human personality out of the inorganic matter which is the brute stuff of which our universe is exhaustively composed – on the atheist view? Can rationality and life spring from chance and non-being? No, the fact of human personality is another impressive pointer to the God who created us in his own image. That is not to say that God is restricted to a personality like ours: but it is to say that the ultimate source of our being is not less than personal. Paul Davies, not himself a Christian, makes this point well:

> The physical species *homo sapiens* may count for nothing, but the existence of mind in some planet in the universe is surely a fact of fundamental importance. This is no trivial detail, no minor by-product of mindless purposeless forces. We are truly meant to be here. The physical universe is put together with an ingenuity so astonishing that I cannot accept it merely as brute fact. There must be a deeper level of explanation.

Where else can we look for that deeper level of explanation for mind and personhood in our world than God?

4. The fact of values

Look at the fact of values. We all have them, but they are very hard to understand if there is no God. After all you don't expect to find values knocking around in molecules! Matter does not give rise to morals. So modern godless people are confused about where our values fit in. We value life – but why should we if life really springs from chance? We value truth – but why should we if there is no ultimate reality? We value goodness – but what is that doing in a world derived from plankton? We revel in beauty – but there is nothing in it, since it too springs from the chaos in which our world originated. We value communication – but the universe is silent. Yes, we have our values, and they do not accord very well with the atheist's picture of the world, sprung merely from chance, matter, and millions of years to allow for extensive development. I do not find much basis for value judgments there.

But what if there is a Creator God? Then life is valuable because it is his greatest gift; hence the infinite value of every individual. Truth matters because it is one aspect of God, the ultimate reality. Beauty and goodness are likewise two of the 'faces' of God, and every good action or beautiful sight is an inkling of the good and beautiful source from which they come. Best of all, we do not inhabit a silent planet: God has spoken and revealed himself, to a considerable extent, in the world, its design, in values and in human beings. When we communicate, it is not vain jabbering, but God-given ability, entrusted to us by the great Communicator himself.

Those are the two possible attitudes to values. I know which makes more sense to me.

5. The fact of conscience

Look at the fact of conscience. That's a pointer to God, if ever there was one. Your conscience does not argue. It acts like a law-maker inside you, acquitting you or condemning you. It doesn't say, 'Do this because you will gain by it' or, 'Do it because you will escape trouble that way.' It just says, 'Do it.' It seems to be a remarkable, categorical pointer to the moral God who put it there. Oh, of course, it is not the voice of God pure and simple. It has been warped by all kinds of things: our environment, our rationalizations, our disobedience. But equally certainly, conscience can't just be explained away as the pressure of society. It was not from any pressure by society that John Newton and William Wilberforce conscientiously fought for the liberation of slaves, or Martin Luther King championed the cause of black people. Their actions were carried out in the teeth of opposition by society, and so it has always been with every moral advance.

Despite the diversity of human cultures the world over, there is actually remarkable agreement on the essential values to which conscience points: the general condemnation of murder and adultery, of theft and lust, of hate and hijacking. There is universal agreement that peace is right and war is wrong, that love is right and hate is wrong – however little we manage to carry it out in practice. And it is conscience that points us to this difference between right and wrong, and the claim right has on us. C. S. Lewis summed it up like this: 'If no set of moral ideas were better than another, there would be no sense in preferring civilised morality to Nazi morality. The moment you say one lot of morals is better than another, you are in fact measuring them by some ultimate standard.' And that ultimate standard is God.

Morality, conscience, the difference between right and wrong, are important pointers to a God who is interested in what is right and good and true. Here is no blind force, no abstruse designer, but a personal God, so concerned with what is right that he has built a moral compass into each one of his creatures.

6. The fact of religion

Look at the fact of religion. We are religious animals. In the sixth century BC, philosophers in Greece poured scorn on religion, and invited people to grow out of such superstition. Religion continued. And so it has done ever since. The Russians tried to abolish religion after the Revolution in 1917. They failed. They tried again with violent persecution under Stalin. They failed. And now the gospel is making massive advances in Russia. Sociologists over fifty years ago confidently predicted that religion would have withered away by the end of the twentieth century. Instead it is the major force dominating world politics. The fact is that people are incurably religious. We are going to worship either God or a pseudo-God, but worship something we will, even if it is something very physical like material prosperity, or something very abstract like the idea of progress.

> There is one fact about man that has distinguished him since his first appearance on earth. It marks him as different from all other creatures. That is, he's a worshipping animal. Wherever he has existed there are the remains, in some form or other, of his worship. That's not a pious conclusion: it's an observed fact. And all through history and prehistory when he's deprived himself of that he's gone to pieces. Many people nowadays are going to pieces, or they find the first convenient prop to tie their instincts to. It's behind the extraordinary adulation of royalty. It's behind the mobbing of TV stars. If you don't give expression to an instinct, you've got to sublimate it or go out of your mind.

Such is the conclusion not of a philosopher or a priest, but a novelist, Winston Graham, in *The Sleeping Partner*. He is right, is he not?

These are some of the facts that, taken together, not only make belief in God reasonable, but make it very hard to deny his existence. They point to a God who is skilful, skilful enough to design the courses of the stars and the development of the foetus. They point to a God who is the source of human personality, and therefore not less than personal, however much he may transcend all that we mean by that word. He is the source of our values: life and language, truth, beauty and goodness find their ultimate home in him. He is so concerned about right and wrong that he has furnished each of his creatures with a conscience. And he wants us to know him and enjoy him, to worship and to live in his company – hence the universal religious instinct of men and women throughout history and all over the world. But he still remains the unknown God – unless he discloses himself. And that he has done.

7. The fact of Jesus

The most compelling reason to believe in the existence of God is Jesus of Nazareth. He claimed to make God known. He claimed that to know him was to know the Father. He claimed to be empowered by his heavenly Father to forgive sins, to accept worship, and to be the final judge of humankind at the end of all history. He claimed that he would die for the sins of the world, and would be raised to an endless life after tasting death for every man. All this is clearly before us on the pages of the Gospels. The existence of Jesus and a good deal about him is, as we have seen in chapter 9, substantiated by Jewish and Roman sources.

The Gospels show that he lived the most matchless life,

taught as no man has ever taught, fulfilled scores of prophecies uttered centuries before, and yes, he was raised after
death from the chill of the tomb on the first Easter day –
what the great ancient historian Momsen called 'the best
attested fact in ancient history'. We glanced at some of the
evidence for his resurrection in chapter 10.

To put it crisply, if you examine the following eight factors
you will get to the heart of who Jesus was. His worldwide
influence, his marvellous teaching, his moral perfection, his
miracles, his fulfilment of prophecy, his claims, his death
and his resurrection add up to a formidable case that he is
indeed the Son of God, the Saviour of the world.

Conclusion

So you don't have to throw your brains away to become a
believer in God. The evidence is very strong, far stronger than
the atheist case. Consider the alternative for a moment.

One of the most pressing questions of the twenty-first
century is this: What is man? Christians believe that men
and women are made in the image of God, and their inherent value lies in precisely this fact. Despite our frailty and
failures, we remain the objects of God's love and he plans to
spend eternity with us.

But once remove God and it all looks very different.
Human beings do not spring from a loving personal source.
As the atheist and Nobel Prizewinner Jacques Monod put
it, 'Man must wake up to his total solitude, his fundamental
isolation. Like a gypsy, he lives on the boundary of an alien
world, a world that is deaf to his music, and is as indifferent
to his hopes and fears as to his sufferings and his crimes.'

Consequently human beings have no inherent value.
From matter we come and to matter we return. 'Man

has no divinely prepared nature to be fulfilled by action,' wrote Sartre with rigorous frankness. 'What is he but a little puddle of water whose freedom is death?' 'Life,' wrote Ernest Hemingway, 'is just a dirty trick from nothingness to nothingness.' And nothingness, of course, is where it all ends. 'On humanist assumptions life leads nowhere, and every pretence that it does is a cruel deceit.' So wrote the very honest humanist H. J. Blackman.

And while he does remain alive, modern atheist man perceives in his own life and in society an increasing collapse in ethics. 'Is there no God? Then everything is permitted,' reflected Dostoevsky. So it is not altogether surprising that Klaus Barbie, the notorious World War Two 'Butcher of Lyons' could claim 'I have done no wrong!' If you do not believe in a personal, ethical source of the world and all that is in it, then nobody should be surprised if moral behaviour gives way to selfish gratification. Ethics becomes simply what I want or think I can get away with. This often happens in individual lives, but it has happened on a massive scale in the past century in the atheist regimes of Hitler's Germany, Stalin's Russia and Mao's China.

Atheism set out to be the liberator of humankind. It emerged in Europe with the French Revolution at the end of the eighteenth century. It was a protest against the corruption of the church and the oppression of the monarchy. But almost immediately, the admirable atheist ideals of liberty, equality and fraternity turned into the mindless slaughter of the Reign of Terror. And sadly in our own day we have come to recognize that it is atheism, not Christianity, which has turned out to be the oppressor of mankind. Atheistic regimes have proved unbelievably oppressive and ruthless throughout the vast territories, amounting to nearly half the world, where they held sway fifty years ago. Millions have been slaughtered for daring to question their dogmas. But the Christian faith has been seen to be the liberator both in the Soviet Empire and most recently in China, where there are now well over seventy million believers. And this is no accident. For real Christianity does not only make intellectual sense of the world and of ourselves: but to share our lives with the author of our existence brings great joy, fosters love for other people, reaches out to meet human need, demands moral living and offers a firm hope for life after death based on the historical resurrection of Jesus of Nazareth. I would not trade my Christian faith for anything this world has to offer. Certainly not for the atheist alternative.

It is hardly surprising that reflecting on the implications of rejecting God leads many thoughtful people to despair. 'Only on the foundation of unyielding despair can the soul's habitation safely be built,' claimed Bertrand Russell, that massively erudite atheistic philosopher. And today's post-modern generation tends to agree. The logic is inescapable. If there is no God, there is no ultimate hope for humankind. No wonder our society, like the Roman Empire in its decline and fall, is consumed with a desire for handouts from the state and exotic entertainment from the media. They dull the pain of a Godless world, but they cannot satisfy. Only God can do that.

APPENDIX

In his fascinating book, *Beyond Belief?*, Nick Spencer explains his examination of the religious views of agnostics. He moderated five groups of eight respondents, diverse in age, gender and social background. Three groups were recruited in London, two in Nottingham, all by professional market research recruiters. The object of the research was to understand the attitudes of the agnostic mainstream that makes up the majority of our population.

Interviewees were recruited according to three main criteria: their (non)belief, their (non)attendance at religious services, and their self-designation (whether they called themselves Christians or not). People who were confident that God exists were excluded, as were those who were confident that there is no God. The remaining 'agnostic' sample covered 66% of the population of Great Britain, according to the Office for National Statistic's *Social Trends 30*.

In order to establish the first of these criteria, recruiters read out to respondents a series of statements drawn from the 1998 British Social Attitudes survey:

1. I know God really exists, and I have no doubt about it.
2. While I have doubts, I feel I do believe in God.
3. I find myself believing in God some of the time but not at others.
4. I don't believe in a personal God but I do believe in a Higher Power of some kind.
5. I don't know whether there is a God and I don't believe there is any way of finding out.
6. I don't believe in God.

Those who were sure that God existed, and those who were sure he did not, were both excluded, in order to access the beliefs of the less certain 'agnostic' mainstream.

Second, people were asked whether they regularly attended a religious service of any kind. Those who did were excluded. The rest belonged to the 81% of the population of Great Britain who, according to the Office for National Statistic's *Social Trends 31* (1999) do not worship as often as once a month.

Third, people were asked about how they would describe themselves – Christians, Jews, Muslims, etc? In the three London groups, all those who laid such a claim were excluded. This was modified in the Nottingham groups because recruiters reported that there was a great willingness among people, despite being agnostic and non-attenders, to call themselves Christians. Though confusing, this is a common phenomenon. The 2001 National Census showed that 72% of the population of England and Wales call themselves Christian, and a further 5% belong to other religions. Only 16% said they had no religion (7% gave no answer). Thus both the London and Nottingham groups represent the enormous fringe constituency which continues to exist in Britain. The Nottingham groups did not go to church, were not sure quite what they believed, but still liked to call themselves Christians, while the London groups came from the more antagonistic end of the agnostic spectrum.

These were the respondents that Nick spoke to as part of his research. They were interviewed according to the three criteria outlined above, in two-hour groups, and were asked about their lives and beliefs, and their attitudes towards religion in general, and Christianity and the church in particular. Some of their responses are contained in the chapters in this book: the rest are in Nick's book, *Beyond Belief?*, obtainable from the London Institute for Contemporary Christianity (www.licc.org.uk). As Mark Greene, the Director of the London Institute observes, the results 'afford a fascinating perspective on early twenty-first-century Britain'.

FURTHER READING

Chapter 1. 'You don't have to go to church to be spiritual'
J. W. Sire, *The Universe Next Door* (IVP, 1977; 4th edn 2004)

Chapter 2. 'The church is just too inflexible'
M. Green (ed.), *Church Without Walls* (Paternoster, 2002)
S. Jones, *Why Bother with Church?* (IVP, 2001)
G. Tomlin, *The Provocative Church* (SPCK, 2002)
Mission-Shaped Church (a brilliant report put out by Church House Publishing, 2004)

Chapter 3. 'Christians are such hypocrites'
C. S. Lewis, *Mere Christianity* (Fount, 2002)
J. E. Hare, *Why Bother Being Good?* (IVP USA, 2002)
M. Keene, *Christianity* (Lion, 2002)

Chapter 4. 'Religious people are too intolerant'
C. Nonhebel, *Don't Ask Me to Believe* (Lion, 1998)

Chapter 5. 'You can't trust what is in the Bible'
F. F. Bruce, *The New Testament Documents* (IVP, 1960, new edn 2003)
R. Burridge, *Four Gospels, One Jesus* (SPCK, 1994)

Chapter 6. 'Science has disproved Christianity'
J. Polkinghorne, *Belief in God in an Age of Science* (Yale Nota Bene, 2003)
M. Jeeves & R. J. Berry, *Science, Life and Christian Belief,* (Apollos, 1998)
D. Ratzsch, *Science and its Limits* (Apollos, 2000)

W. Dembski, *The Design Revolution* (IVP, 2004)

A. McGrath, *Dawkins' God: Genes, Memes, and the Meaning of Life* (Blackwells, 2004)

Chapter 7. 'There's just too much suffering in the world'

A. McGrath, *Why Does God Allow Suffering?* (Hodder, 2000)

J. Jones, *Why Do People Suffer?* (Lion, 1993)

M. Meynell, *Cross-examined* (IVP, 2001)

Chapter 8. 'There are too many religions in the world for them all to be true'

M. Green, *But Don't All Religions Lead to God?* (IVP, 2002)

M. Goldsmith, *What About Other Faiths?* (Hodder, 1999)

Chapter 9. 'There's not enough proof for me to believe'

J. W. Sire, *Why Should Anyone Believe Anything At All?* (IVP, 1994)

N. T. Wright, *Who was Jesus?* (SPCK, 1992)

Chapter 10. 'Something 2,000 years old can't be relevant to me today'

F. Morison, *Who Moved the Stone?* (1930; Authentic Lifestyle, 1996)

J. Anderson, *Evidence for the Resurrection* (IVP, 1950)

Chapter 11. 'If there is a God, why doesn't he just send someone down?'

A. McGrath, *The Unknown God* (Lion, 2002)

M. Green, *Who is this Jesus?* (Kingsway, 2004)

Chapter 12. 'That is all very well, but I'm not sure I believe in God'

A. McGrath, *The Twilight of Atheism* (Doubleday, 2004)

P. Williams, *The Case for God* (Monarch, 1999)

G. Carey, *The Great God Robbery* (Collins, 1989)

Other possible books

J. R. W. Stott, *Basic Christianity* (IVP, 1977)

J. I. Packer, *Knowing God* (Hodder, 1993)

NOTES

Chapter 3
1. Matthew 6:2, 5, 16; Luke 12:1.

Chapter 4
1. Luke 9:49–50.
2. Matthew 5:38–39; Luke 6:29; Matthew 26:51–53.
3. Matthew 12:9–14; Mark 3:1–6; Luke 6:6–11; 14:1–6.
4. Matthew 15:1–20; Mark 7:1–23; Luke 12:37–39.
5. Matthew 21:12–13; Mark 11:15–17; Luke 19:45–46; John 2:13–17.
6. Matthew 16:21; Mark 8:31; Luke 9:22, 51.
7. Matthew 27:11–26; Mark 15:2–15; Luke 23:1–4, 13–25; John 18:28 – 19:16.
8. Matthew 18:20; 28:20.

Chapter 5
1. Mark 12:36; John 5:37–40.
2. Matthew 5:17–18; Mark 12:24; John 10:34.

Chapter 6
1. Genesis 1:14–19.

Chapter 8
1. John 10:30; 14:7–10.
2. John 14:6.
3. John 6:35; 15:1.
4. Mark 4:39.
5. Luke 7:14–15.
6. Mark 6:38–44.

7. Mark 2:1–12.

8. Mark 10:45.

9. See 1 Peter 2:24; 3:18.

10. Hebrews 10:14–18.

11. Romans 3:24–26.

12. See, for example, the resurrection accounts in Matthew 28; Luke 24; John 20; 1 Corinthians 15.

Chapter 9

1. John 20:24–31.

Chapter 10

1. Romans 1:4.

2. Mark 10:33–34.

3. John 20:6–7.

4. 1 Corinthians 15:6.

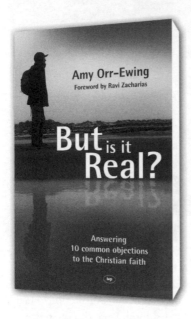

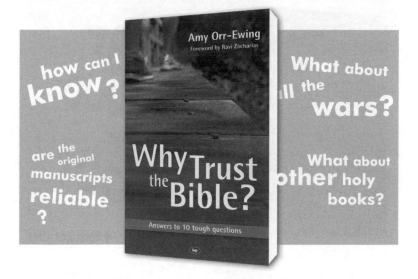

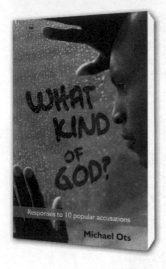

www.ivpbooks.com

For more details of books published by IVP, visit our website where you will find all the latest information, including:

Book extracts   Downloads
Author interviews   Online bookshop
Reviews   Christian bookshop finder

You can also sign up for our regular email newsletters, which are tailored to your particular interests, and tell others what you think about this book by posting a review.

We publish a wide range of books on various subjects including:

Christian living   Small-group resources
Key reference works   Topical issues
Bible commentary series   Theological studies